WEST MARIN DIARY

WEST MARIN DIARY

John Grissim

ISBN: 0-912449-35-7

Published by:
Floating Island Publications
P.O. Box 516
Point Reyes Station, CA 94956

On the cover: The author *aprés* surf in the land of cows and cowabunga. Photo by Michael Sykes.

On the titles pages: "Point Reyes & Drake's Estero." Photograph by Marty Knapp.

Back cover photograph of the author by Judi Buckley.

All other photographs in the text by the author unless otherwise noted.

Illustrations by Kathryn LeMieux, pp. 7, 25, 52, 68, 75.

Illustrations by John Francis, pp. 12, 31, 93, 102, 126, 127.

BY THE SAME AUTHOR

Country Music – White Man's Blues. Paperback Library, New York, 1970

We Have Come For Your Daughters. William Morrow, New York, 1972

Billiards – Hustlers & Heroes, Legends & Lies, and the Search for Higher Truth on the Green Felt. St. Martin's Press, New York, 1979

The Lost Treasure of the Concepcion. William Morrow, New York, 1981

Pure Stoke. Harper Colophon, New York, 1983

For Susan

CONTENTS

ix / Foreword
xi / Introduction
3 / Western Lore
5 / Bo Bo — City of Contrasts
8 / The Duxbury Incident
10 / Unplugging
13 / One Man's Great White Hope
16 / A Boy and His Gun
18 / Small-Town Sharks
21 / The Secret of the Firemen's Ball
23 / Of Porn, Uzis, and Sin City
27 / The Black Angel
29 / Splitters West of the 'Plug
32 / Of Love and Harvest Moons
34 / The Weekly Miracle
36 / Bob Dylan's Stinson Visit
39 / Don't Go Near the Water
42 / The Eternals
44 / The Real Story
47 / A Bolinas Confessional
50 / Manna for the Soul
53 / The Fires of Winter
55 / Dumping With Dignity
57 / Storm Run
59 / Getting to Huey
62 / Felony Fishing
64 / Risk Taking, Thanks Giving

66 / Incident on a Winter's Night
69 / How I Made Peace With Television
71 / Those Innocent Ice Picks
73 / Respite in the Water
76 / My Night as Doorman
78 / Our Little Town
80 / Floating Island
83 / The Great Gadget Revolt
85 / Dinner for the Alums
87 / Storm Surfer
90 / Highway 1 Traffic Solution
92 / Fog Mantra, Fog Laughter
94 / Super Gopher
97 / Super Gopher's Strange End
99 / The Secret of Dillon Beach
101 / Uproar in Dillon Beach
103 / Quiet Change
105 / The Raging Columnist
107 / Kitty Day
109 / Typewriter Memories
112 / The Barrel in the Mist
115 / Camping With America
117 / The Commander Checks In
119 / West Marin From a New Angle
122 / Talking in the Doorway
124 / West West Marin

"Bob Dylan at Ed's Superette. The mind boggles."
Oil on canvas by Michael Knowlton. *(See p. 36.)*

Foreword

It was a mid-January night in Stinson Beach, and writer and adventurer John Grissim sat by his fire brooding on the state of his life – and in particular, how it was affected by the television set in his front room. "Even when turned off and blank," Grissim eventually observed, "[the TV] seemed no less an intrusion than when turned on."

Outside a gale was howling, and Grissim, like a latter-day Lear, began to rage about the hearth. "I sensed the onset of a fine madness. . . . Abandoning my seat before the hearth, I pulled on my waders, shrugged into my foul weather jacket, and with a certain rough relish, pulled the 40-pound [television] from its corner perch. Outside, the storm raged as I dumped the set into the trunk of my car and headed for my destination. . . . The waves were huge, and the on-shore gale screamed as I strode purposefully to a deserted portion of the beach, lugging the set into the heart of a nasty night. Wading out into the swirling foam, I dropped the TV into shallow water and stepped back a few paces. Seconds before a large wall of white water engulfed the machine, I aimed a revolver at the screen and fired. The tube imploded with a noise I can only describe as thoroughly satisfying."

That's almost the end of the story. Grissim remained TV-free for a year or so and, for awhile at least, novels by Joseph Conrad and Arthur Conan Doyle occupied the TV's space in the corner. The only epilogue is that the next morning, Grissim returned to the beach and gathered up the demolished set for proper disposal. Now there's an environmentalist in gonzo clothing.

Grissim told the tale in the Jan. 21, 1988, edition of the weekly *Point Reyes Light*. He's been a *Light* columnist since early 1984, recounting tales of small-town life and coastal culture. A man of many interests, Grissim has also written books on surfing and billiards, and has crewed on a successful treasure hunt in the Caribbean. He has written the screenplay for an erotic film and has interviewed rock stars for *Rolling Stone*. The "California Living" section of *The San Francisco Examiner* on March 24, 1985, described Grissim as a "guy [who] has knack for being where the action is – as long as the action involves adventure, riches, beautiful women, fast cars, billiards, rock 'n roll, fishing, and certain other pastimes." The same issue carried Grissim's interview with porn star Marilyn Chambers in which she talked about her life's work and her new fondness for Uzi machine guns.

While all this makes for wonderful entertainment, there's more to Grissim's writing than just excitement and action. Judging from his columns in the *Light*, I would say some of Grissim's best writing has been done while alone in a studio next to the woods, as he ruminated on modern man's quest for bucolic bliss. Grissim is fond of the small-town characters he writes about, and he tells their stories sympathetically. It's an endearing side to this journalistic adventurer, and more than a few of his female readers have told me they are secretly in love with him.

As editor and publisher of *The Point Reyes Light*, it is my responsibility to get his column edited and in the paper in a timely fashion, and in fairness to John, I should note he's never missed an issue. But I do recall a few stretched deadlines – including the time he was so late he felt compelled to arrive at the newspaper in a new and very expensive Maserati, which he was test driving for a magazine story. Grissim insisted on taking me for a spin around the block, arguing: "You'll probably never get another chance." I knew the ride was a diversionary tactic, but I went along. After seven years of working with Grissim, I've come to recognize his adventures usually make for grand stories.

– Dave Mitchell, editor & publisher
Point Reyes Light

Introduction

In early 1984, when I suggested to Dave Mitchell, editor and publisher of the *Point Reyes Light*, that I try my hand at a weekly column, I was pleased with his encouragement — and a little nervous. True, I had lived a decade in West Marin as a peripatetic writer and journalist, but I wasn't at all sure I had it in me for more than a half dozen outings. Nor had I a name for the column. Several weeks passed. Finally, I devised a strategem to lessen guilt in the event of failure, insisting I not be paid for the first few columns — and took the plunge. I soon discovered that writing from the heart is actually a fairly straightforward procedure: one sits down at the keyboard — and opens a vein.

More than 400 columns have appeared since then. Looking back, I'm quite amazed that I never missed a deadline (though there were close calls) but I suspect the reason owes to two powerful motivators. One is the pride of being associated with a Pulitzer prize-winning newspaper widely regarded as one of America's best country weeklies. And the other is the *Light*'s readers.

Every time I prepare to write "West Marin Diary" I envision the faces of many of the more than 12,000 people who each week read the *Light*. In the past eight years I've shared much of my life with them, for my column is indeed a diary. They not only have taken me seriously, but their affirmation and loyalty encouraged me to take risks, to reach for the best in me, even to the extent of occasionally leaving a touch of crimson on the page. Their trust has meant a great deal to me.

I am indebted to eleven readers in particular who believed that a collection of my columns deserved to appear in book form, and who, together with my esteemed editor Dave Mitchell, put up the money to underwrite a first edition. They are:

Jack and Ethel Aldridge, Don Beacock, John Edwards, George Flynn, Ron Grunt, John Jones, Bill Kent, Richard Kirschman, Jim Mitchell and Lisa Adams, David Plant, and Josiah "Tink" Thompson. These good people represent an astonishing diversity of backgrounds, ideologies and achievements. I am honored and profoundly thankful that they joined together in this project.

In working on the book's production with Michael Sykes, editor and publisher of Floating Island Publications of Point Reyes Station, I have gained a first-hand appreciation of why his is one of the book industry's most respected small presses. From the initial discussions with David Mitchell and me (abetted by a decent Merlot), to shooting the cover photo, through the typesetting, design, selection of art work, and page layout, Michael's creativity, meticulous craftsmanship, and infectious enthusiasm were an inspiration. Please see the column titled "Floating Island" elsewhere in these pages.

I am indebted to John Francis, the celebrated Planet Walker, for his many fine pen and ink sketches drawn during his stays in West Marin, and to Stinson Beach artist, surfer, and old friend Michael Knowlton for the black and white prints of his vivid paintings. Susan Robinson did a superb job of meticulously proofreading the final layout. Thanks also to Kathryn LeMeiux, creator of the nationally syndicated strip "Lyttle Women," for many of the miniature end-of-column icons known affectionately in the printing trade as "dingbats."

Lastly, a confession. When I began "West Marin Diary" I harbored a secret hope that a soul mate might be out there waiting, a woman who followed my adventures, my angst and my laughter, who read between the lines, and who because of these things would some day wish to know me. That happy eventuality indeed came to pass, resulting in my timely exit from the lonely surfer fast lane and on to a path more adventurous than any I've ever taken.

From my heart of hearts I thank all of you who have made it possible for me to share in these pages some of those experiences.

John Grissim
May 1991

WEST MARIN DIARY

Judy Borello, owner of a Point Reyes Station landmark that is one of the great authentic cow town saloons of the American west.

WESTERN LORE

EARLY ONE EVENING awhile back I was nursing a beer at the Old Western Saloon when I noticed something odd about the illuminated stained glass fixture above the mirror behind the bar. That's the one that looks like half a Tiffany lampshade with letters spelling "Western" on the side. Several letters were missing. And the frame was pretty well bent up. Looked like someone had really nailed it with an airborne bar stool—maybe missing somebody in the process.

When I asked the bartender (Rhonda or Amber, I wasn't sure whom) about the damage, she smiled thinly and said, "Well, we're not really talking about it." Her reply, of course, poured gas on the fire. I immediately imagined a feud between town heavyweights, perhaps over a lady, which triggered a fist-fight that became a brawl. Actually, I later learned, nothing quite that romantic had transpired.

Seems one of the well-liked locals walked in one night holding a Two Ball Inn beer mug and reportedly announced that he'd always wanted to bust a bar mirror. Whereupon he let fly with the mug. Bystanders reckoned the reason he clean missed the mirror and instead hit the stained glass was because he appeared to be two sheets to windward and listing about 10 degrees to port. Hell, that's gotta throw off a fellow's aim.

Fortunately, owner Judy Borello understands that accidents can happen. She later called him and told him she could either go light or heavy. He said, "Light, please," apologized profusely and ponied up the cash to have Mike Mezaros, the Inverness fire chief and a fine craftsman, restore the fixture. Mike did a bang-up job, and everybody felt the whole affair was handled in a right neighborly fashion.

Judy, who has owned the Western for 10 years (husband

Bob owns the building), has a strong sense of saloon tradition and knows much of the Western's past. Fact is, she's writing a book about the bar's history, hoping to some day publish an illustrated volume tentatively titled "The Old Western Rides Again."

The other afternoon, as she installed old 78s in a vintage 1945 juke box, she shared a few gems of Western lore. For example, years ago when she removed the false ceiling over the bandstand she found dozens of bullets embedded in the woodwork. During the 1940s, she explained, a lot of cowboys used to pack iron and regularly used the alcove ceiling lamp for payday target practice. During that same era, the local sheriff's deputy often used the liquor storeroom in the back for the overnight lock-up.

Judy has a fine feel for legend and has even figured in a few episodes in recent history. Back in the late '70s, for instance, during parade day on Western Weekend, about 50 riders belonging to, not one, but three rival motorcycle clubs showed up at the Western and parked their bikes en mass along the curb. While town fathers worried outside, the Sons of Hawaii, the Sidewinders, and the Vampires made themselves at home inside. Judy, sensing the undercurrent of intramural rivalry, quitely invited the leaders of the three clubs to a conference by the pay phone.

"Fellas," she said, "We're happy to have you here, and we want you to enjoy yourselves, but if any of you are fixing to fight, I expect you to take your business outside."

"Ma'am," replied one of the leaders, speaking for all three, "We'll go you one better. We've declared the Old Western neutral territory. And if there's to be any fighting, we'll take it two miles outside of town."

The three clubs were models of decorum for the duration. The Western since became a favorite rest stop for clubs out on weekend runs. Once, when a visiting delegation from the East Bay learned it was Bob Borello's birthday, a trio of ladies riding with their dudes sang a splendid a cappella version of the R&B song, "Happy, Happy Birthday, Baay-bee."

Recently, a visiting English tourist confessed to Judy he was amazed to find a saloon in which cowmen, rednecks, fishermen, longhairs and truck drivers all seemed to get along famously. That such informal laissez faire exists here in West Marin says something about the folks who live here. And the Western provides a classic saloon ambience, from its stained glass right down to its matchbooks decorated with a red rose, a derringer and a garter. In fact, especially the matchbooks.

The only other saloon that comes close in the realm of such amenities (in my experience, at any rate) is a Nevada saloon/maison de joi whose matchbooks have a similar old western design, on the backs of which is printed "The Sweetness of life lies in dispensing with formalities."

But I digress.

March 8, 1984

BO BO—CITY OF CONTRASTS

JUST KIDDING, FOLKS. I wanted to see what that would look like at the top of the column. Actually, this is about Downtown Bo Bo which last Friday night was packed and jumping, largely because of the dance at the Community Center. Featured were the Michael Roach Band and Roger & the Fast Lanes, both polished homegrown groups that played to a very appreciative crowd, about half of which hailed from Stinson.

Roger Lane was especially sharp, fronting a tight four-piece band and coming across as a self-assured, smooth, flippant, brash, funny, hard-working pro. That guy plays everything well: the lead in "South Pacific," baseball for Smiley's A, poker, pool, and Pac Man. He's one of the most zestful characters around.

Smiley's was wall-to-wall, of course. Over the shouting, bartender Charsell Hopper said Smiley's was one of only 14 California bars more than a century old. Charsell was even featured in an AP story about vintage saloons that appeared about the same time as did that *N. Y. Times* story that mentioned Pluto and his car-lot home. Funny, none of the locals raised a fuss about unwanted publicity. Maybe things are changing.

Smiley's Schooner Saloon is one great bar. Over the years it's been the setting for a few classic moments. Like the night in 1976 when I snuck in the women's world runner-up pool player, intending to watch her clock the local hot sticks. She was doing all right until "Star Trek" Seth took off half his clothes and threw them on the table, insisting that Scotty beam him up. A minute later she tripped over a German Shepherd and her opponent, Arthur Okamura, ran five and out. She never recovered.

A year later Jon Goodchild, Jim Anderson and I brought Julie Christie there. Owner Sue Bradley didn't recognize her and carded her. Ah, the stuff of legends.

When the present owner Robert Glen took over, he commissioned architect Steve Matson to rehab the joint. Steve and friends did a terrific job, preserving the ambiance while installing enough hardwood to render the place literally bulletproof. Since then there have been no serious fisticuffs. Some say the clientele is changing.

It's hard to tell. These days one sees a fair number of Stinson folks there, even as the Sand Dollar has become an occasional hangout for Bo Bo locals. Hands across the lagoon. The desire for social variety among singles in their 20s and 30s is probably the reason. If the Sand Dollar, with its rugs, fireplace and pub ambiance, serves as a community living room, then Smiley's with its pool table is the club house. It's a nice mix.

One senses a mood shift in Bo Bo, or at least the anticipation of change. For example, after the great oil spill of 1971 when an influx of bright newcomers settled in and linked ideologies with the resident poets, there followed fermentation and tumult. The California vision of Ecotopia may have been born here. That elegant volume, *The Town That Fought To Save Itself* (by Orville Schell and Ilka Hartmann) was one of several gems that resulted.

However, after the tenth set of Bolinas highway signs disappeared, I remember thinking the book might well have been titled, *The Town That Dared Not Call Its Name*. Yet, in the last decade, it seems that many of the movers and shakers have moved on, while their places have not been taken by others with a similar zeal, expertise and vision. Granted, the platform stance remains intact and the Border Patrol is still a media presence, but most of the generals have retired or moved on. A sign of the times?

Howsoever one may interpret these developments, it seems that Bo Bo these days is a little less angry. To be sure, for every redneck elsewhere in these parts, there may be a corresponding Bo Bo astral fascist to keep the faith with occasional public outbursts of livid righteousness (though no names come to mind at this writing). Could it be that the inexorable forces of rising property values and the Bed & Breakfast boutiquing of West Marin now lay claim to the future? If so, the impact of such a trend bears close scrutiny.

The town of Bolinas (as distinct from Downtown Bo Bo) would certainly merit examination in this event. To that end I have made application to the Consulate for a visa. Gee, I don't know what all the fuss is about. Paul Kayfetz has graciously assured me that as soon as I tell him the desired date of my visit, he will make all necessary arrangements for my passport. Stay tuned.

April 12, 1984

THE DUXBURY INCIDENT

THIS WEEK been windy enough for you? Can't say I've ever seen a gustier seven days in May. The worst appears over, however, which must come as a relief to the charter salmon boat skippers who can now return to the fish-rich waters around the Duxbury buoy. Bolinas fisherman Josh Churchman should find the going easier, too. I hear tell he's been picking up a few good-sized halibut in the net he sets just inside the reef.

Actually, this season Josh has had to contend with more than wind. The other day something very big slammed into his net and tore several fathoms to shreds. Josh knew right away what had happened—a shark (most likely a Great White) had nibbled on some of the stuck fish, then shrugged off the net as though it were no more nuisance than a cobweb. Small demonstrations like this are one reason why West Marin fishermen and surfers have dubbed the local variety of shark "the landlord." Or "the man in the grey flannel suit."

There's something fascinating about these awe-inspiring critters. And many's the time I've listened to locals brainstorm various ways to snare a Great White. Their schemes are partly motivated by money since San Francisco's Steinhart Aquarium has a standing offer of $5,000 for any six-foot Great White shark delivered F.O.B. alive-and-well. Such a modest length, you might figure, would render feasible the task of catching a specimen. The only problem is that young Great Whites grow so fast that they're only six feet long for about 12 hours.

To give you an idea of just how chancy the shark-catching game can be, consider a recent incident from the annals of local fishing lore. A few years ago Josh Churchman happened to mention to Stinson marine sculptor Peter Allen that he had made several sightings of great whites cruising the four-fathom waters inside Duxbury where there is a natural break in the reef. Peter, who had never seen a living great white, decided this might be a fine opportunity to catch one in relatively safe waters. With luck, he would subdue the fish unharmed and turn it over to the Steinhart.

Having extensively studied the great white while making numerous wood carvings of sharks, Pete had a good idea of the tackle he would need. Accordingly, he teamed up with fishing buddy Steve Lewis and devised a rig composed of a 20-pound Danforth anchor attached to a 55-gallon oil drum with 40 feet of steel cable from which were suspended five Mustad hooks roughly the size of the curve you can make with your thumb and ring finger.

On these Pete and Steve impaled the carcasses of rock fish. The pair hopped aboard Pete's 17-foot aluminum salmon skiff, went out through the Bolinas lagoon channel to the cut in the reef, and plopped the rig in the water. They then returned to shore. And waited.

The idea was to keep an eye on the barrel float and if it started moving or bobbing in the water, they would jump aboard and rush out there and wait alongside until the shark had fought itself to exhaustion. Night came with no perceptible change in the barrel's position. The next morning at dawn Pete and Steve returned to the scene and gingerly pulled up the gear and stared wide-eyed at its condition.

All five hooks had been cleaned of bait and were as straight as toothpicks.

When word spread around the lagoon of the incident, Pete's father Howdy (a longtime outdoorsman and environmentalist) caught the bug and took up the challenge. Howdy's first move was to up the ante.

He went to a blacksmith in Point Reyes Station and ordered a humongous hook made of stainless steel. The distance between barb tip and shaft was the length of a man's forearm. Other elements were beefed up: a 25-pound anchor was used, the cable was braided stainless wire as thick as lamp cord, and a second float (this one a 2½-foot-diameter ship's mooring buoy) was attached by a 10-foot wire to the 55-gallon drum.

When everything was ready, the Allens and Steve Lewis returned to the reef, baited the hook with a garbage can full of old fish, and set the gear in place. The trio returned to the beach, having instructed Allen Sproul, who at that time lived on the Bolinas mesa overlooking the reef, to keep watch with binoculars.

Once more night fell with no noticeable change in status. Come dawn the next day a wind swell had sprung up but the three fishermen gamely charged out to the reef to inspect the gear.

It had vanished. Lock, stock, barrel, and buoy. Gone without at trace. The three returned to port mystified, humbled, and not a little shaken by the experience.

May 17, 1984

UNPLUGGING

THEY HAVE a lovely home high in the woodsy hills of Mount Tam above Four Corners. Off the kitchen is a mossy brick patio beneath cool redwoods.

And sliding doors lead from the living room to a spacious deck with a grand view. Oddly, there isn't a stick of furniture on either the patio or deck, but then this busy professional couple had only lived here six months.

Oh, I did see in the backyard a satellite dish right next to the directional TV antenna. The system brought in 120 channels with fantastic reception, they said, showing me the large screen set into the living room wall cabinets. Arrayed on either side was an elaborate stereo system, cable couplers, a VCR, and a large collection of records, cassettes and videotapes. And a pair of Sony Walkmen for when they went running or biking.

I remember thinking how there was once a time when young couples used to have kids. Nowadays they have lifestyles.

"We just love being here in the trees," she said. "It's so quiet and rustic, and we're so glad to be finally out of The City."

I was musing over these things at dusk one recent evening as I trimmed the wick on my Aladdin kerosene lamp. Striking a kitchen match, I touched the wick and watched the flame slowly crawl around into a circle.

Over the flame I set the silk mantle and the thin, elegant glass chimney. The flame made tiny guttering sounds as I adjusted the level. Then silence. In a few seconds the mantle blossomed into a white gold radiance. The room seemed to bask in its soft glow — as did its occupant.

A very pretty piece of work these Aladdins. They're a bit high strung and require intelligent handling, but with a couple of them around the cabin I have the freedom to literally unplug from the rest of the world. And slow down. And feel the fullness of this West Marin land.

Of my Mill Valley friends with their satellite access to the world I intend no criticism. They are children of the electronic media. And, to some degree, so am I by virtue of earning my living with a pen. Yet I confess that, given a choice between the dish antenna and a kerosene lamp, I'm partial to the latter, for it is far richer in memory and connotation.

As a youngster I remember my father breaking out the kerosene lamps when big winter storms hit the coast, knocking down power and telephone lines and leaving whole communities on their own. For several precious hours our family, momentarily isolated from the larger world of school and work, would gather around those lamps to eat our meals, play Monopoly and cards, and read aloud and laugh, and, most of all, be a family.

I recall the excitement of donning my yellow, oiled canvas raincoat and a pair of galoshes with their black metal boot clips and following my father out into the wind and lashing rain to bring armloads of oak logs from the garage back into the livingroom where the lamps were burning. It was thrilling.

In the years since there have been other times when a kerosene lamp has evoked similar feelings. Like lying at anchor in Drake's Bay aboard a friend's sloop and playing backgammon in the galley after a dinner of fresh-caught salmon. Or taking a couple of kids night fishing for leopard shark in the Bolinas

Lagoon. Or learning by experience how perfectly suited a lamp is for lovers when there is otherwise absolutely no need for one at all.

It is because of such happy memories that I feel a warmth and an excitement from the simple act of touching match to wick. A bit escapist, I agree, but it is certainly one of the more harmless paths to a respite from the cares of a workaday world. For me it is a part of the art of unplugging.

Apropos kerosene lighting, a few years ago Stinson musicians Peter and Lorin Rowan wrote a memorable song for my musical "Mysterious Doings In Rinso Bleach." The character who sang the song was Candy Uforia, a fast-lane Mill Valley siren who came to Rinso Bleach to break a few hearts but who instead fell in love with the place. The opening lines:

"I remember the thrill, / when I first came over the hill, / I was a vamp, / I was so camp, / now all I have is a kerosene lamp."

And sometimes, Candy, that's all you need.

July 5, 1984

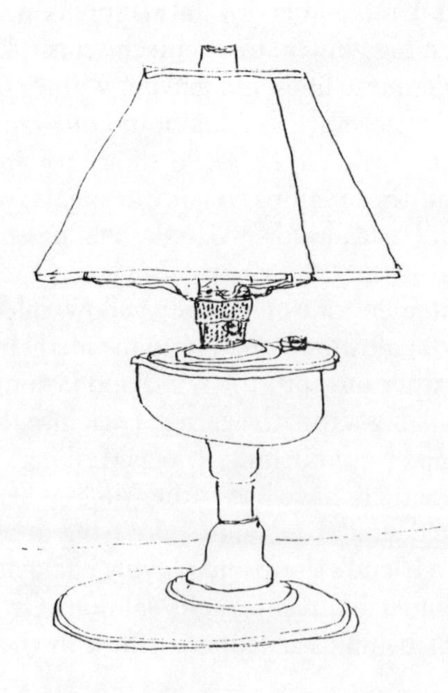

ONE MAN'S GREAT WHITE HOPE

LAST FRIDAY, when Bolinas commercial fisherman Josh Churchman found a live, male, 200-pound baby great white shark six feet long enmeshed in his halibut net near the Duxbury Reef, he had little idea what a curious chain of events his remarkable discovery would set in motion – and of the impact of those events on one Stinson Beach resident in particular.

When Josh returned to Wharf Road that night, word of his catch quickly spread. Within minutes Smiley's Saloon emptied and the dock became a noisy circus as two dozen spectators vied for a look at the creature. The shark appeared quite weak since the only way Josh was able to safely bring him back was to tie a rope around his tail and slowly tow him through the channel. The shark's backward movement prevented oxygenated water from flowing into its mouth and gills, the result being the fish was half-dead from suffocation.

Hoping to save the fish for the Steinhart Aquarium, Josh called several friends for help, among them fisherman Rudy Ferris and Stinson marine sculptor Peter Allen, who rushed to the scene. The two made a makeshift sling to turn the fish 180 degrees so it faced into the current of the outgoing tide.

In the meantime the shark had become the focus of Bo Bo's ecotopian street politics as several bystanders, heedless of the fact that Josh has a family to support, argued the fish should be cut loose. Sometime near midnight, after an exhausted Churchman had gone home, some astral fascist boarded his boat and cut the shark loose.

It was nearly 2 A.M. that night before word of the release reached a shocked Peter Allen, who raced back to the dock. Together with Alex Horvath (hastily recruited from the last-call crowd at Smiley's) he hopped into a rowboat and began a flashlight search.

For Peter Allen the mission was of special significance. Long before he became an artist whose wood sculptures of fish and marine mammals earned him an international reputation, Peter was an outdoorsman, fisherman, surfer and conservationist whose father taught him never to kill anything he didn't intend for the dinner table.

As he matured as an artist, Peter's renderings of sharks — in particular the great white — won him highest praise, even though he had never actually seen a live one until last Friday.

For years Peter acknowledged that sharks have both fascinated and terrified him. He became a lay expert in shark lore, an informal advisor to fishermen, park rangers and naturalists. Yet to spend hours each day meticulously sculpting these sinisterly beautiful creatures was to reap his share of dark dreams.

And now here he was suddenly thrust into the night aboard a flimsy rowboat peering among the pilings in the low-tide silence of the Bolinas Lagoon, praying he would find something he heretofore hoped he would never face — a dorsal fin moving through water.

They say a hot sweat takes it out of the fat but a cold one takes it out of the soul. Adrenalin flowing, Peter spotted that fin among pilings and trailed it towards Kent Island before losing sight. Moments later, after disembarking to walk the muddy flats of the island, Peter paused to scan the water, then almost as an afterthought, looked down.

There, barely a yard from his feet, lay the shark, nosed in at right angles to the shore, its huge sabre-like caudal fin slowly moving from side to side.

It was an encounter Peter later described in terms bordering on the spiritual. And understandably so, for here at last, after 30 years of wondering and studying and dreaming about this incredible fish, this nearly mythic leviathan that he had long feared and loved, Peter now faced it in the flesh.

In a strange way that wonderous fish had come to him as an offering, a gift, the fulfillment of one man's hope. In that extraordinary moment of communion between man and beast, Peter knew it was dying. Knew, too, that if by some miracle it went on to live in the lagoon, the results could be devastating.

Thus it was with a mixture of great sadness, compassion, awe, and a touch of primordial fear that Peter, with Alex's help, gaffed the shark and put it out of its misery.

Yet because of Peter Allen, who has carefully preserved for study the tail, fins and head of that magnificent great white shark, it will in a special way live to see many lives.

July 26, 1984

Bolinas fisherman Josh Churchman's ill-fated baby white was less fortunate than this female specimen caught in the flounder nets of Tomales's Al Wilson in August, 1980 and rushed to the Steinhart Aquarium. She lasted four days before becoming confused and weak. The Steinhart released her at the Farallon Islands, but not before she became front page news world wide and was seen by 40,000 people who waited hours in line for a peek. Photo: Jeff Lee.

A BOY AND HIS GUN

I HAD TURNED 11 a few months before that Christmas day when my parents gave me my first rifle. It was a .22 caliber Remington model 514 bolt-action, single-shot — and as I held it proudly I sensed I had reached a plateau of young manhood. I remember well those early mornings before breakfast when my father took me into the Marin hills to shoot at cardboard bull's eye targets. Indelible memories — of the tearing crack of a shot in the chill air, the smell of cordite when pulling back the bolt to eject a shell, the voice of my father as he carefully explained gun safety, and perhaps most of all, a special father-and-son closeness.

For the next two years that Remington was my proudest possession, and I became a fair hand as a marksman. When Frank, a business associate of my father, gave me a birthday subscription to the *American Rifleman* magazine, I began learning about guns and hunting.

I learned that animals such as raccoons, skunks, ground squirrels, jack rabbits, and prairie dogs were generally referred to as "varmits." And that it was great sport to go out to farms and ranches and get clean, accurate kills from great distances, especially using a scope-mounted rifle.

One Saturday dad's friend Frank drove us to Bass Lake here in West Marin to do a bit of sport shooting. As we stood on a road that looked down on the lake, Frank pulled out a beautiful .220 Swift rifle with a 4X scope, leaned over the hood of the car, and took careful aim at a seagull resting on the water in the center of the lake. The bullet shattered that bird into a dozen pieces, sending up an eruption of white water. We laughed.

A moment later Frank took aim at a turkey buzzard directly overhead. Again a loud report; the bird exploded into confetti and fell cartwheeling to the ground 200 feet away. "Boy," we said to Frank, "that sure was some kind of varmit shooting."

That summer I stayed at a ranch near Mendocino for a few weeks. I brought my rifle to hunt raccoons. We would take empty beer cans and, using a can opener, punch all the way around the top so that the resulting teeth bent inward. Then we would pour syrup into the cans and attach them with wire to a ground stake by the garbage pile. After nightfall we'd wait behind a woodpile 50 feet away until we heard the unmistakable sounds of a panicked raccoon struggling to pull its paw out of the can. Then we'd turn on the flashlights taped to our rifle barrels and open fire. We got two or three varmits that way.

Back home in Marin I seized on a similar tactic to catch a raccoon, this time using a powerful spring-loaded leg trap which back then a 13-year-old could easily buy at any sporting goods store. At dusk one evening I tied raw bacon to the trip-lever and gingerly placed the trap under some tree roots on a creek bed not far from Phoenix Lake where earlier I'd spotted paw prints. After nailing to the tree trunk the end of the 10-foot chain connecting the trap, I rode home on my bike. That night I slept fitfully.

At first light the next morning I returned with my rifle to check the trap and was astonished to find a large female raccoon with her bloody paw caught in the trap. As she frantically pulled at the chain, madly clawing up the tree trunk, then dashing into the creek, I desperately took aim and fired. The bullet chipped off the tip of her shiney black nose.

For a second the raccoon stood motionless, and for the first time in my life I saw the face of fear and suffering, and the ghastly look of a being that knows it is trapped and about to die. Again and again I shot, until finally she fell on her side, quivered a moment, then lay still.

I returned home with my prize, proud and excited and flushed with victory, yet sensing deep within me that I had been the willing instrument of a terrible tragedy. That afternoon after school I returned home to skin my trophy and soon realized to my horror that I had killed a raccoon that obviously had been nursing a litter of newborns.

It took months before the full impact of the desperate minutes of that killing sunk in — and years before the shame and the sorrow gradually merged into understanding and acceptance. But not since that eventful day have I ever hunted or killed anything for sport.

Strange. As I write this, a magnificent three-point buck and his doe are grazing circumspectly a mere 50 feet from my studio window. He's looking my way now.

His nose is shiney and black.

September 20, 1984

SMALL-TOWN SHARKS

ALL THE TALK about sharks these days brings to mind a few encounters I've had with a certain species of West Marin shark that prowls the murky waters around that green island of high seriousness commonly known as a pool table. Now, I've logged my share of time stalking the tables at the Old Western, and spent many an hour fingering the felt at Smiley's, but recently my most memorable set-to's have taken place in the Stinson Beach firehouse which now boasts a table for the use of the volunteer firefighters.

Come to think on it, the table itself was sort of famous in West Marin even before we acquired it. A few years ago, when the department voted to buy a used table, I was volunteered to find one, seeing as I'd recently authored a book about pool hustlers titled *Billiards: Hustlers & Heroes, Legends & Lies, & the Search for Higher Truth on the Green Felt.*

My search led me to the McIsaac ranch in Tocaloma, home of young Allen McIsaac, a self-taught phenom who was rumored to have won weeks earlier close to $20,000 playing eight-ball against a Lake Tahoe building contractor.

When politely asked about such a marvelous achievement, Allen unconvincingly denied the report, then grinned sheepishly

when I complimented him on his new shiny, black Pontiac Trans-Am with a gold phoenix on the hood. He did, however, own a vintage slate table which he had set up in a cold, drafty storage room in an old milking barn. The felt was covered with plaster chips and bird droppings, indicating Allen hadn't used it for some time. That figured, since my book research revealed that as soon as a kid gets a taste of good money earned with a cue, he loses all interest in practicing alone at home. But the table itself was sound and Allen was pleased to see the table find a new location where it would be appreciated.

No sooner was the table installed (complete with new felt) than from out of nowhere appeared a few hot sticks who until then had kept a low profile. I was pleased with this development since I secretly fancied myself a fair cue-handler. I was also prone to lecture about the values of meditation and concentration when deeply engaged in a difficult match.

There's a lot to be said about concentration. It works, it appeals to advocates of clean living, and it's almost patriotic. Alas, I have since learned that utterly dissolute behavior on occasion produces similar results. I have watched someone who hasn't picked up a cue in years knock back a few shots of high octane spirits and flat-out dust the competition.

A case in point is famed Stinson local George Frayne, a.k.a. Commander Cody, noted rock star, artist, and bon vivant, who claims he once played his college English teacher for a passing grade. "That's absolutely true," he insisted one night at the Sand Dollar. "It wasn't that I was stupid at English, but the class was held at 8 a.m. Saturdays and that conflicted with my lifestyle."

Since Cody rarely gets on the table here, one evening I egged him into a three-out-of-five session of nine-ball for $20. Having knocked back two Becks and a double shot of schnapps, he readily agreed. As the two of us walked to the firehouse with a dozen onlookers, I realized I had just challenged a veteran rocker who (1) had just played a dozen sold-out gigs, (2) was riding high after an acclaimed TV guest shot on the David Letterman Show, (3) had just downed two boilermakers, and (4) was convinced he could shoot the lights out. I sensed a shark attack.

"Grissy, it's all over," Cody barked after winning the toss.

"In fact, even if you won, you couldn't win."

He took the first game handily, broke the balls again and ran half the rack before I got in – and missed. The Destruction Derby continued as he moved briskly around the table with non-stop patter, easily winning the second game. A rout was in the making. Either I fired up or all was lost. I was desperate.

Suddenly the fire phone rang with a report a car had skidded into the lagoon. Casting my cue aside I climbed into the squad truck and fired up the engine. Cody, whose frequent out-of-town travels prevent him from joining the department, stood by the table amidst noise and exhaust fumes, yelling "Hey!" What about the game?"

"Sorry!" I shouted. "We'll have to reschedule!"

Firemen swarmed into the station. More engines started. As we pulled out I looked back to see Cody waving his cue and shouting, "Grissim, you turkey! Come back here!"

But he was laughing.

October 11, 1984

Commander Cody closing in for the kill: "Grissy, even if you won *you couldn't win."*

THE SECRET OF THE FIREMEN'S BALL

It was a classic vignette: It's Monday morning of last week and Stinson Beach Fire Chief Kendrick Rand is explaining to Mildred Sadler, the revered grande dame and Keeper of the Keys to the Community Center, that "We've got this great surprise band for the Firemen's Ball this weekend." Whereupon not one but two giant moving vans pull up to the front doors and disgorge four husky roadies.

While Kendrick and Mildred chatted amiably inside the Center, which can accommodate maybe 280 people in a pinch, one of the roadies hefted a Black & Decker drill with a screwdriver tip and walked to the master light control panel. With four quick "Brrrupps" he deftly removed the holding screws, then lifted away the entire face plate from the wall. While Mildred recoiled from the shock, the roadie, one Richard Watts (son of the late Alan Watts), explained he was merely checking the wiring to ensure it could safely handle the amperage. "Trust me," Richard quipped. "With a name like 'Watts' I'm in the right line of work."

And thus began a hectic week of preparations for the 1984 Stinson Beach Firemen's Ball, culminating last Saturday night with the surprise appearance of Pablo Cruise, a Marin County band that emerged in the late '70s as one of the most successful rock groups in the U.S. and whose records sold millions. The local angle is that a few years ago two members of the band, pianist Cory Lerios and guitarist David Jenkins, bought homes here at the beach. Recently the two remaining original members of the group, bassist Bud Cockrell and drummer Steve Price, joined the line-up. In a much appreciated gesture of community support, the group generously agreed to a surprise benefit appearance at the ball.

Surprise indeed. Hardly had Mildred recovered than the crew muscled in Cory's seven-foot, white Yamaha grand piano and hefted it onto its own carpeted stage.

Added to this were four keyboard synthesizers, a drum computer, two 10-foot-high speaker stacks, and a serious array of remote-controlled gel lights, and you'd have thought the band was gearing up for the Oakland Coliseum. "Wait'll we move in the main equipment," Cory deadpanned. "This little stuff here is just our rehearsal gear."

And rehearse they did all last week. When asked why so much diligence in preparation, drummer Steve Price grinned: "Can you imagine failing in your own home town?"

As Saturday approached the volunteers grew apprehensive about a possible mob scene, even with the publicity blackout. But we were not without experience in such matters. Last year another esteemed local, George Frayne (*aka* Commander Cody) was the surprise headliner, and the ball was an outstanding success.

Shortly after noon Saturday, however, the focus of events shifted to other matters as Stinson emergency crews rolled to the high cliffs over Red Rock Beach. A dozen rescuers, including state and national park rangers, medical technicians, and paramedics treated a young woman whose leg had been severely crushed by a huge log rolling in the surf. By the time we called in a helicopter to evacuate the stricken woman, it was almost time to get ready for the ball.

Well, dear reader, it was a killer night. The Tuesday Night Band, an assemblage of local teens who perform Count Basie big band tunes, played an excellent half-hour set. Then Pablo Cruise took the stage, at which point none other than super-star rocker and local-boy-made-good Huey Lewis bounded on stage and introduced the band. The place went bonkers.

Pablo Cruise opened with "Love Will Find a Way," one of their biggest hits, and never let up, mixing great new material with vintage classics such as "A Place in the Sun," "I Go to Rio," and "Zero to Sixty in Five." Clearly one of the highlights of the set was Bud Cockrell's vocals on "I'm a Rock 'n Roller," performed for the first time since the band has regrouped with the original line-up. Somehow 400 to 500 people caught their act without creating sardine madness. Off to one side Huey Lewis visited with old Stinson chums like Scott Dill while star-struck teenage girls stood by respectfully giving Huey meaningful looks.

Meanwhile, ambulance corps member Frankie Accardi quickly sold all 200 of the blue T-shirts specially made for the occasion. On the front of each is the Pablo Cruise palm tree logo. On the back is "West Marin Tour, Stinson Beach Firemen's Ball 1984." Definitely a collector's item.

As the long evening wound down, my brother Tony, who had driven up from Monterey with his lady to catch the show, summed up the day nicely. "Gee, John," he said, "we've only been here half a day, and all we've done is watch a dramatic helicopter cliff rescue, see Pablo Cruise perform, and meet Huey Lewis. Doesn't anything much happen around here?"

November 29, 1984

OF PORN, UZIS, AND SIN CITY

IT FELT A TRIFLE ODD to be standing in the dark in the pouring rain at 6:30 A.M. on a recent Thursday waiting for the commuter bus from Bolinas. But then I was anticipating a rather odd and eventful trip over the hill. The day before, my editor at a Sunday feature magazine had determined that porno star Marilyn Chambers—she who had recently been nabbed during the now-infamous O'Farrell Theatre panty raid following her burlesque show—would make an excellent profile story. And I was immediately directed to fly to Las Vegas, Marilyn's home for the past 10 years, and interview the 32-year-old actress.

On the way to the airport I thought over my interview topics but sensed my list of questions would eventually boil down to at the most two: 1) Gee, how can you do all that stuff in front of cameras and everything? and 2) What do your parents think?

My plane touched down in Las Vegas shortly after noon under bright crisp skies, and I was met by Kim, a svelte Japanese girl with long red fingernails who introduced herself as Marilyn's secretary. She drove me to a bustling gun shop and survival store in which, she explained, Marilyn and her manager have an interest. Right, another profitable lower chakra investment.

I met Marilyn in The Survival Store's office, following which we drove in her black '83 Volvo turbo to an Italian restaurant. While we lunched over chef salads she was asked three times to sign autographs. Wearing a beige, V-necked flared dress she looked snappy. When she spilled a dollop of salad dressing on her chest, she dipped a napkin tip into her Perrier (the woman no longer drinks) and vigorously cleaned away the spot, in the process loosing only her listener's complete chain of thought.

As for my two questions, Marilyn laughed and said she's been a show-off and an exhibitionist all her life and she's always liked it and, besides, she's only made five porno movies in 15 years. As for her parents' feelings, she confessed they have never, ever wanted to hear a single word about the career in adult films that has made her one of the top two or three names in the biz.

We never got around to going horseback riding (as had been suggested before I left California) but it was a fun interview. Sometimes I felt as though I were talking to a bright, articulate kid sister, and at others I felt slightly intimidated sitting next to an awesome porn actress. When I mentioned the latter sensation, she readily admitted she gets the same reaction from people when she's at social gatherings. Right, it gets lonely up there.

Later that evening, after Marilyn dropped me off at my hotel on the strip, I noticed the Smothers Brothers were headlining the Riviera Casino next door. On a whim, I saw the show and wrote a note to Tom Smothers (an old acquaintance who lives near Sonoma), mentioning I was in town for one day from Stinson Beach. I lavishly tipped the rather stiff maitre d' (just like in the movies) to deliver the note backstage and was tickled when, 20 minutes later, he returned all smiles (just like in the movies) to say my ticket and drinks were complimentary. After the show, I paid my respects to the brothers and returned around 2 A.M. to my garish hotel room with its sunken tub and cottage cheese ceilings. Las Vegas is, quite simply, ridiculous.

The next morning a smashing girl named Cindy picked me up and drove me to The Survival Store (I was beginning to like this town) where I was introduced to a fellow named Bob, the resident weapons expert. When he invited me to test fire anything in the store, I immediately chose the Israeli-made Uzi. Bob led me to the indoor firing range and gave me a thorough lecture on this machine gun (which fires 800 rounds per minute on full automatic). During the few seconds it took to convert $50 worth of 9mm bullets to a lot of noise (on full auto, of course), I was lost in a macho fantasy having to do with a daring rescue at the Entebbe airport. I think Marilyn was billed for the ammo.

Late that afternoon I returned to San Francisco and took a cab to the O'Farrell Theatre and walked into the lobby in the middle of a full-on police search for evidence. I quietly withdrew and returned to Stinson Beach, relaxed over a martini at the Sand Dollar and allowed as it had been an interesting 36 hours. Life's a bitch.

February 21, 1985

This chilling photo-illustration by photographer Jeff Newberry accompanied the story "The Haunting of the Black Angel" in the California Living section of the Sunday Chronicle-Examiner, *and proved a major boost to his career as a successful advertising photographer.*

THE BLACK ANGEL

A STRANGE NAME for a roadhouse. Fact is, the burned-out structure that sits on the edge of the salt marsh off Shoreline Highway just north of Stinson Beach has never carried that name. However, a goodly number of locals, including many who have passed on, have long referred to the place by that name. The reason: they are quite sure that there is something in there, a presence that is cold and black and so malefic that its behavior has caused many sober citizens to rethink completely their concept of evil.

We are not talking here of a cute little poltergeist that makes mischief on Halloween, or some grieving Greta whose gossamer form shows up on your Polaroid snapshots. Rather, "it" is a presence that suddenly appears behind you, dropping the air temperature 15 degrees, sending a slight breeze through rooms with no open doors or windows, a black hole that seethes with a powerful magnetism that attempts to draw you into its chaos, its hatred, its insanity.

No, I didn't believe it either. At first. During the roadhouse's last incarnation, as the Over the Hill Bar and Grill (1979–1981), I shared a lot of good times there and heard some great music from the likes of Peter Rowan, the Edge, Merlin and Maria Muldaur. It wasn't until later that I learned the premises had been the target of one cleansing ritual and one full-blown exorcism performed by a priest and four devout parishioners.

Nor did I learn until later that then-owner Kenny Gordon, who for a long time lived in the upstairs apartment, spent long months battling this nightmare presence and ended up with his health nearly destroyed. Or that his long-time friend Marty London (who'd taken a break from her physical therapy practice to help manage the business) was convinced "that thing in there" drove her to ulcers and alcoholism (from whence she has happily recovered and now heads the local AA group). Or that the late Friday Ouselle, who owned the place from 1954 to 1963, had always said no one could make the place a success because it was haunted. Or that some believe that one-time owner Ted Danz (a strange, gifted, eccentric, and tormented man) was driven by the presence to blow the back of his head off with a shotgun in 1978.

Right, this is not some mischievous poltergeist.

How did all this get started? Seems the name "The Black Angel" was provided in the fifties by the late Joe Avila, a Stinson local from whose Portuguese Catholic background the name sprang with the ring of appropriate myth and authority. Joe reckoned the place was haunted after stories got around regarding cold spots in the building, and taps on the floor at night, and candles that mysteriously re-lighted. At first it was all sort of a joke.

Intrigued by these tales, I began this past April to research the roadhouse and its strange history. Local legend has it that the building stands on an old Miwok Indian burial ground and during WWII was once used to temporarily hold Japanese detainees destined for camps in Sonoma. Not true. Actually, it was built in 1937 by Frank Periera as a dance hall and community center. During the war, the Coast Guard leased it for barracks, following which it opened as a bar and grill.

Over the years it changed ownership many times and was variously named the Surf, the Red Whale, and The Brig. In the late seventies, it almost opened as the Reef, then the Pacific Midway Bar and Grill. And finally, the Over the Hill Bar and Grill. Based on a number of interviews I conducted for a magazine story, the presence on the premises appeared to gather strength from any form of negative energy that was around to feed it.

How strong? Consider just one story from Kenny Gordon: "Before we opened, I hired a contractor to install molding and a half-inch pipe bar across the men's room window. The morning after, the bar, the molding and the screws — everything — had vanished. I had another bar installed and again it disappeared overnight. It was unbelievable. Again and again I tried. We used two-by-fours, we used four-by-fours, we used unpullable nails.

There was no way those barriers could be removed except from inside with a wrecking bar. I tried a dozen times before giving up."

Is The Black Angel still in there? Yesterday I drove by the building. Its doors and windows are boarded up with plywood.

Except for the men's room window.

August 8, 1985

SPLITTERS WEST OF THE 'PLUG

"I KNOW IT'S SHORT NOTICE, but would you be up for a two-day shot? I could run solo but after eight years I just don't like being out there alone."

That was Pam Cobb calling from Sausalito last week, just prior to driving to Bodega Bay where she currently lives aboard the Pursuit, a handsome 33-foot commercial salmon troller she's leased for the season. Her deckhand would not be able to make the trip.

"You're on, Pammy," I quickly answered. Whereupon I threw together a change of clothes, donned boots and a watch cap, and prepared to be chief cook and bottle washer for the only woman salmon boat skipper in the Pacific fleet—and an old friend.

An off-and-on Stinson Beach resident, Pam is a classic—early forties, petite, and with very fine straight blond hair that hangs in bangs over a tanned face that alternately glows with exuberance and laughter or clouds over with indecision or worry. With her penchant for wearing necklaces, earrings and rings with fish motifs, Pam always looks feminine and fashionable, even when wearing foul-weather gear. In fact, during the off-season when she works as a legal secretary at the Embarcadero Center, one would hardly suspect she is a respected and seasoned mariner who has been profiled in *Pacific Fishing*. All of which she pooh-poohs because the only thing that matters this time of year is King Salmon.

Thus it was we found ourselves traveling that night through Point Reyes Station, Tomales, Valley Ford and on into Bodega Bay, a serious fishing village whose principal watering hole, the Tides Restaurant & Bar, closes at 10 P.M. because almost everyone gets up at 4 A.M. We were no exception.

Come 6 A.M. the next morning, the Pursuit nudged out past the jetty entrance with its forlorn fog horn and headed west towards a weather buoy nicknamed "the sparkplug" for its similar appearance. As the sun splashed over the eastern hills, a slab of bacon sputtered in a pan on the galley stove, its smell mingling with that of the coffee. In the Pursuit's tiny wheelhouse, I made mounds of buttered toast, while Pam stood at the helm surrounded by a forest of electronics: radar, Loran, two CB radios, one VHF radio, an RDF indicator, a chart fathometer, and a depth indicator, while on the cluttered console before her was a small vase of cut flowers.

Three hours of cruising found us in calm seas 15 miles off the Marin/Sonoma coast. There Pam rigged stabilizer fins over the sides and dropped the trolling lines in 480 feet of water. Her movements were practiced, graceful, and showed the easy economy of motion which veteran sailors unconsciously master. And when that first 20-pound king salmon came over the stern, she shouted with grand high humor and exultation. That magnificent fish, fierce and proud (even in death), represented her lifeblood, her passion, and a shared communion with a deep and ineffable mystery. I, too, felt it.

Pam brought aboard nine fish this day, most of them were "splitters" over 15 pounds—too big for restaurants and thus destined to be split down the middle and smoked.

At one point Pam pulled in several fat red snappers, which I promptly fileted and threw in the oven with the potatoes. An hour before sunset we sat outside in warm sunshine in the stern well feasting on baked red snapper swimming in butter and lemon, baked potatoes with sour cream, fresh steamed garden string beans, and sipped wine spritzers. And all the while the diesel engine droned and the dark blue sea rolled, and the radio crackled with fishermen's banter and gossip, and we, for a brief moment, relished our momentary freedom from the cares of our world ashore.

It was after dark as we gingerly made our way back to Mason's Marina, using a hand-held spotlight to see the channel markers. Within minutes of tying up, I climbed into the fo'c'sle where my bunk promptly hit me in the face. There are few pleasures to compare with the exquisite fall into well-deserved sleep after an 18-hour day afloat.

And fewer still that equal the experience of harvesting the sea when Nature herself conspires to offer up such a rich bounty.

August 22, 1985

OF LOVE AND HARVEST MOONS

I KNOW OF NO ONE who lives out here who hasn't commented at one time or another about that grand view of West Marin that one sees as one descends from Mount Tam down Panoramic Highway to Stinson Beach. It seems no matter what thoughts may be vexing the soul at the moment, that first sight of the confluence of Pacific Ocean and unspoiled land rarely fails to elevate the spirit. Many times, at such moments, I have sighed and said aloud, "So good to be home." It's a kind of sentimental mantra.

Sunday evening as I returned from an afternoon over the hill, my mood was bordering on maudlin as I rounded the bend and once again drank in the homecoming vision. I was returning from a Mill Valley party of mostly media and designer types, having felt oddly out of place in my jeans and OP sandals. Nice people, but their generally somber clothes and sallow complexions reminded me of the bumper sticker on the van belonging to Dino Columbo who manages Kirby Ferris's surf shop: "Work is for people who don't know how to surf."

It must have been the music and the full harvest moon that conspired to envelop me in a sweet, sad longing. Nature provided a glorious rising moon, while the tape deck played "At the Vanities," a 1934 movie theme beautifully embroidered by a Gershwin piano and soaring strings. There in Bolinas Bay a dozen salmon boats lay snugly anchored, awaiting the last day of commercial salmon season. In the far distance, a marshmallow carpet of fog rolled across the Bolinas mesa, leaving visible only the laconic flashing red light from the tallest of the old RCA antenna towers out by Commonweal. And below me nestled Stinson Beach, glowing with street lights that bespoke reassurance — everything's still peachy in Rinso Bleachy.

My mood was not one of self-pity, but a longing was there nonetheless. A longing to experience once again the feeling of being in love. Awhile back I was introduced to a woman who, during the course of the following hour of conversation, utterly captivated me with her intelligence, accomplishments, humor, carriage, and vivacity — in short, she pushed all the right buttons. As I marveled at each facet, as I felt each epiphany burst like small explosions of light within me, I felt deep within my heart the first stirrings of soul love. You know the feeling — beyond sex, beyond lust — glimmerings of the Big One, that high-stakes romantic explosion that gives one that junkie rush of Love.

Even as I felt these wondrous stirrings, I struggled to temper them — for the very good reason that she was married. I have no idea whether she sensed any change in my demeanor. I saw none in hers. There was nary a hint of flirtation, never a suggestion of encouragement. I liked that, too.

A heart could trust a woman like that.

Following this singular encounter I felt thankful that I had at least experienced a hint of the subtle power of a certain kind of love, and glad to know that "They're still out there." And,

Stinson Beach overlook. Oil on canvas by Stinson Beach artist Michael Knowlton.

God willing, I'm still hanging in here. To be sure, searching for the love of one's life isn't the be-all and end-all of existence, but part of me is like the coyote in the desert – not patiently hunting but actively waiting, lurking behind that cactus, ears perked, eyes scanning, and ever ready to act upon the vaguely occult knowledge of what I sometimes call the Exquisite Sniff.

It is fun on occasion to indulge oneself in such maudlin moods, to wallow in the moonlight of unrequited limerance. For there are seasons to all things, even for harvesting love. The dog-eared copy of the *Farmer's Almanac* which lays on my bedside bookshelf assures me of these things, especially of the caprice of this fall season, my favorite. "Nature gives bounty and variety but it seldom gives consistency," says the *Almanac* for this month. "Rather, what we see of it is full of trickery and contradiction – to all of which we respond at least as gratefully as we do to order."

Perhaps that's why, in this world of caprice and inconstancy, the lonely heart within all of us can rejoice on a fall day at the view from Panoramic. For indeed, it's good to be home.

October 3, 1985

THE WEEKLY MIRACLE

FOR THIS REPORTER, this issue of the *Light* marks the end of a six-week-long foray into the world of newspaper journalism as it's really practiced. Which is to say, during the absence of our esteemed editor and publisher, who dashed off to Europe for a much-needed vacation, I, for two days each week, sat in his chair in my capacity as junior copy editor and re-write man.

Now, as flattered as I was that Dave asked me to fill in, I confess I never told him the closest I'd ever come to actually doing real newspapering was when I edited a laid-back monthly surfing magazine in Sydney, Australia for a few months—in which instance deadlines took second place to waves. Nor had I ever taken a single course in practical journalism.

"Don't worry," Dave soothed. "Rhonda Parks will have everything under control. Just help her with a few minor tasks. Like here, for example—with this column-width story you want to go to 20 picas wide and use either a 12 Helvetica Bold or a TC 36-point head with a scant 22 count. Got that?"

With a touch of anxiety, I nodded, at which point Dave continued breezily: "You'll be using my computer here. Just slip in a double-formatted program disk, follow the prompt codes to access your B disk files, and use Wordstar to do your writing. Then use Spell-Check for confirmation, slap on a coded slug for correct interfacing with the Compuset, and you're all set." Ever the helpful fellow, Dave handed me 10 pages of hints on computer use—10 pages of single-spaced items using such phrases as Warm Boot, Bad Sector, B-DOS Error, and Escape Lock-out. God help me if the computer ever decided I deserve that last distinction.

I mean up to that point I could talk computers, but I'd never actually sat down and used one, for heaven's sake. So of course I said, "Hey, no problem, Dave."

Looking back, I don't remember too much about that first week except I garnered some understanding why newspaper people seem to develop a fondness for booze. Good Lord, if it wasn't the importance of the 4-H club meeting, it was the crush of little kids with zucchinis waiting for their photos to be taken. If it wasn't phone calls about cliff rescues and seaweed seminars, it was last minute write-ups on benefit dances, sports, and senior wellness workshops—every one of them of considerable importance to all kinds of people out there. And, believe me, you'll hear from them if you get it wrong.

Clearly, a few things became obvious to me. For starters, this newspaper, no matter what you might think of it, is damn important to a community of people of whom I've never been that aware. It also has a life of its own that is close to mystical in its implications, by turns a beast, slave-driver, and angel. In a real way, it is a weekly manifestation of a collective community consciousness, and as such generates great passions. Being a part of this process can get in one's blood.

And to think I almost got fired only once. Actually, the feeling of family I felt in the *Light's* offices was remarkable, especially for someone used to working alone with no one to talk to but an occasional deer passing by my studio.

It is during the deadline press that some small but gratifying moments occur. I loved watching Rhonda talk very professionally over the phone, then hang up and shout, "That S.O.B.!" Or seeing photographer Dewey Livingston saunter out of the darkroom with an award-winning print of the Point Reyes Lighthouse. And, most of all, being on hand when a fresh edition comes back from the printer and we all grab a copy and devour it. And, each in our own way, pausing to marvel that somehow the miracle once again happened. Thanks, Dave.

October 17, 1985

BOB DYLAN'S STINSON VISIT

Peter Rowan, a longtime compadre whom I met years ago when I first moved to the beach, called this week to say howdy and catch up on the gossip. A fine musician, singer and songwriter, Peter has been in the business for two decades and is the composer of "Panama Red," "The Free Mexican Airforce," and recently, "You Make Me Feel Like A Man" for country super-star Ricky Skaggs (currently No. 7 on the charts). Peter now lives in Nashville but he misses life here at the beach where he lived during most of the '70s.

While talking of old times, I reminded Peter that it must be just about ten years ago when, on a sunny Sunday afternoon, Bob Dylan paid him a visit to look over his mandolin with an eye to buying it – and to pick a few tunes. Peter laughed as he recalled that singular encounter.

It happened that Dylan, who was then wandering alone

around the country more or less incognito, dropped in on Bolinas' Ellen Sander, a former New York rock writer who'd known him in the '60s. Ellen was thrilled, of course, and when her visitor mentioned he was looking to buy a mandolin, Ellen sent Dylan to Stinson, preceded by a phone call.

The scene shifts to the funky second-floor apartment of Selmer's barn on Calle del Ribera. Leslie Rowan, Peter's wife at the time, hung up the phone saying "That was Ellen Sander saying she's sending over some guy who says he's Bob Dylan to look at your mandolin." No one present took the advisory too seriously, including guests Milan Melvin and his wife Bonnie, veteran music cognesenti. A half hour passed before the phone again rang. This time Peter answered. When he asked where the caller was, Dylan replied "Ed's Superette."

Dear Reader, can you imagine Bob Dylan at Ed's Superette? Can you imagine Bob Dylan just saying "I'm at Ed's Superette"? The mind boggles.

Peter provided further instructions to his soft-spoken caller, hung up, and waited. Ten minutes later a Dodge panel van pulled into the narrow Calle leading to the beach proper.

Peter Rowan cutting up on Mount Tamalpais for a publicity photo that became his record logo and a poster image for several bluegrass and folk festivals.

Leslie Rowan, peeking through the curtains, watched a skinny guy of medium height climb slowly out of the van. He wore a dark corduroy suit, engineer's boots, and a matching engineer's cap (also of corduroy) and dark glasses. "Well, he's about the same size as Bob Dylan," Leslie remarked. "And his face looks like it might be Bob Dylan's," Peter said. "And that's probably what Bob Dylan would wear," Milan Melvin added.

A minute later there was a soft knock at the upstairs door. Peter went to the door and introduced himself. When Peter invited him in, his visitor declined, asking if the two of them could go somewhere and pick. Peter nodded, excused himself, got his mandolin, and told Leslie and company that "Bob and I are gonna pick a few tunes in the meditation room downstairs." In reply to their silent question, he shrugged and grinned.

The two musicians repaired to a small studio and meditation room and began swapping tunes. And sure enough, it was Dylan. He accepted a can of Coors and, after hearing a couple of Peter's songs, broke out his guitar and sang, "Tangled Up in Blue," and "Shelter from the Storm," both from the then-yet-to-be-released LP *Desire*. It was your basic all-time thrill.

"There were no lights in the room," Peter recalled. "And we were both wearing dark glasses. As it got darker and darker I kept wondering if Dylan would take his off. Pretty soon I could hardly see myself but by then it had sort of come down to which cool dude was going to be the first to remove his shades. It got pretty funny."

At that point Peter's younger brother happened to pop in. "Oh, Bob," said Cool Dude Peter casually, "this is my brother Lorin." The two continued picking, at which point Dylan played a new tune, "Jack of Hearts." By then Lorin had flashed on who "Bob" was and a minute later he himself played "Old Silver" from his first Rowan brothers album. Peter chipped in with "The Ballad of Joaquin Murietta," a cassette of which his visitor insisted he send him immediately, hinting he might want to put in on his next album.

It was after dark when Peter and Lorin walked to the van with Dylan, ending an incredible three-hour exchange. Did he ever take off his dark glasses? "No, he never did," Peter confessed. "An amazing display."

Peter decided not to let go of his mandolin but invited Dylan to come on out to the beach anytime to look it over.

Bob Dylan at Ed's Superette. The mind boggles.

December 19, 1985

DON'T GO NEAR THE WATER

IN ALL, the episode lasted about four hours on a balmy May 7th evening in Stinson Beach. For some, the occasion was an impromptu block party on the hill, for others a time of bundling small children and pets and valuables into cars and seriously wondering if this time "It" would finally happen. At one end of town laughter and excitement, at the other grim evacuation.

Ironically, I was driving home down Mt. Tam, having just delivered a magazine article about sneaker waves, when I heard the news about the Alaskan earthquake. I wondered whether events to follow would impell me to rewrite the story. And yet I was excited. Who wouldn't be? To witness from a safe distance a "tidal wave" would be a once-in-a-lifetime experience. As I have admitted previously in this space, I love a disaster as long as nobody gets hurt.

During the four years in the 1960s when I lived on Oahu, tsunami warnings were taken seriously. For my friends who had boats at Honolulu's Ala Wai Yacht Harbor, a warning meant call a few friends, rush to the boat, get underway, and be safely a half mile offshore by the time the wave arrived. And be sure to stop for a bottle or two of wine on the way down to the harbor. Here at the beach a great many souls, having no yacht harbor to run to, dashed to the Sand Dollar instead.

Before dinner I was already fielding long distance phone calls from friends in Houston and New York. I explained to them that, if a significant seismic sea wave (to use the formal term) did hit Stinson, it would likely begin with a hardly noticeable one-foot rise in the existing tide, followed by this amazing phenomenon of the waters of Bolinas Bay dropping by about 10 to 15 feet over a period of 15 minutes, leaving fish flopping and crabs crabbing, and the air filled with an eerie stillness marked by the striking absence of beach waves.

As the crest of the tsunami arrived, all that water would roil and roll in and over the beach – not necessarily as a giant crashing wave, but rather as an unruly, foaming, very fast tide that would rise at the rate of two feet or more a minute. That water could do a fair bit of damage as it rolled over Seadrift and down the Calles and Patios, eventually coming to rest against the hillside. Shoreline Highway around the lagoon might be four feet under water.

For three, perhaps four, minutes, that water would remain standing, sloshing around like water in a bathtub. Then, as the tsumani's trough arrived, all that water would begin rushing back into Bolinas Bay. What was left standing would be pretty well devastated.

Now the above description is pretty frightening, but it is not based on a worst case scenario. Moreover, a wave only half that high would still be rough. The key thing to remember is it's not always the incoming water that gets you; it's the outgoing. Which is why I had to smile when, during the evacuation of the Stinson lowlands last Wednesday evening, the dispatcher for County communications came on the air and asked the Stinson Fire Department to "closely monitor the beach water level for any abnormal change." Fire Chief Ken Rand dutifully acknowledged the message, then after a pause, replied, "Frankly, Comm. Center, I don't think anyone here will be down there checking."

Fellow volunteer firefighter Douglas Buckley and I manned one of the fire trucks that made the rounds. Town residents were quick to respond. I could see the reflection of the truck's flashing red lights in the windows as people grabbed what they could. A stream of cars poured through Seadrift Gate. Above the noise, I could hear Park Ranger Bill Wilson's dry monotone PA announcement: "All personnel are urged to evacuate to higher ground." I felt like I was in an old sci-fi B-movie: "Whatever you do, don't touch the blob! Don't look at it!"

Our efforts managed to flush out several fabulous looking women whose presence enlivened the Sand Dollar's ambiance. One of them was worried because she'd left behind her birth control pills. In all, everything went very smoothly. "It" didn't happen, but you couldn't have asked for a better preparedness drill. Later, as we put the fire truck away, Buckley grinned and quipped, "Boy, this sure is an exciting town to live in."

Right. Even when, sometimes, you can't go near the water.

May 15, 1986

In February, 1983, when huge once-in-a-century storm surf inundated Stinson Beach, this cute sea lion pup ended up 200 yards inland on Calle del Embarcadero asking for directions in front of a dump truck that had just carried a load of riprap to Seadrift. Assistant Fire Chief Kenny Stevens and I gently corralled the critter with visquine and lifted it onto the back of a fire truck for transfer to the Seadrift boat ramp. Enroute we bonded with the little fellow and with sad hearts shooed the pup into the waters of the lagoon. Photo: Barry Stebbings.

THE ETERNALS

"WE ROLLED FOR PINTS and spoke of William Blake and the eternals . . ." That line from Van Morrison's song came to mind as I drove north at a scenic pace along Tomales Bay. Big Blue was taking the turns nicely, the way a '74 Ford LTD was meant to—easing into the curves without staggering, then exiting with the leisurely grace of a turkey vulture catching the updraft while looking over a potential dinner. To speak of Blake and the eternals is to ponder those weighty poets who themselves pondered the eternal questions—of the meaning of existence, of the purpose of the storms and gyres of life. I was in such a mood.

A thick fog abruptly appeared over Inverness Ridge, and after a brief hesitation to reconnoiter, began a cavalry charge down and across the chill wind-whipped bay. I could afford to rejoice in the gloom, for I was listening to a soaring piano concerto on an FM station that was coming in clear as a crystal wine glass. And I had slipped into a grand melancholy that was aching and lonely and yet thrilling and grand and civilized. Here was sadness that comes with embracing life, not retreating from its vicissitudes.

Matters of the heart were on my mind. Until recently I had spent virtually every weekend for four months with a wonderful woman. We had spoken daily on the phone. We became close friends. We each kept a caring eye on future possibilities. Then, within a period of 10 days, we both realized we had become wonderfully close friends who, at bottom, weren't in love with each other. So we stopped seeing each other. No tears, no heartaches, no jealousies or arguments. No one on the short end. We still adore each other. Damndest thing you ever saw. Such a denoument has never happened to me before.

Still, I have not looked forward to resuming the hunt (or should I say active waiting). It was a Sunday brunch with friends where I was introduced to a potential new development. Sounds like a real estate deal. She was a trifle aloof and testy, I was offhand and not really trying. The old romantic in me wanted to take one look and feel heavy chemistry, to be smitten and giggly — and otherwise not have to try.

There were the little tests. She ordered a soda and bitters. Oh, God, maybe she doesn't drink. She later switched to a Bloody Mary. No one at the table smoked. Did I dare admit I am notorious for bumming ciggies from friends at the bar? That I sometimes buy a pack to leave in the drawer below the cash register? Two others said they did aerobics and went places on bicycles. But not she. Whew. She dressed down. I liked that. She laughed when someone said her recent ex was the kind of fast-track achiever who used words like "focus" and when he said hello maintained eye contact just a trifle too long. She wore black Reeboks, I had on Argentinian suede cowboy boots. A tie. Who was keeping score? I was in a high school.

At Tomales I turned onto the Dillon Beach road and ambled through heavy fog past sheep ranches, past ancient grape stake pasture fences covered with green lichen, past two-story Victorians with gabled front porches that spoke of a once prosperous, bustling town that once vied for the county seat. The FM station had shifted to a 12-voiced Gregorian mode appropriate for my passing by an entrance way on either side of which were imposing granite monoliths which shared the heavily carved words "Catholic Cemetery." I wondered when the word cemetery had replaced the "graveyard." Doubtless, early boosterism on behalf of the undertaking lobby. Correction, morticians.

The mind beginning to swirl like the fog around Blue. Echoes of Hitchcock movies, premonitions of mortality, the unceasing passage of time, the pain and sometime joy of the eternals. Then back to Sunday brunch. Conclusion: we had checked each other out intellectually. Neither of us had evidenced the enthusiasm of the hunt. Or, for that matter, the subtle business of active waiting.

I continued meandering through delicious fog in my warm

Blue cocoon, eventually reaching Valley Ford, home of my esteemed mechanic Bill Henke who crawled out from under a 10 wheeler to shake hands. "Things have changed," he explained. "My rate is now $35 an hour. But if you watch, it's $45. If you help, it's $55. And if you worked on it first, it's $85."

Actually, things haven't changed. Bill Henke is still a maestro with a wrench, and he still takes time to observe a meadow lark inspecting a bird house he just erected in the backyard, and to nod approval over matters of spring and the pace of the season.

It was a good day for Blake and the eternals.

May 22, 1986

THE REAL STORY

A man named Grissim tried to jump off a fifth floor balcony with a bottle of gin, but he was restrained by police, then forced under a cold shower in the hospitality lounge. His friends and associates laughed as he was taken away in a neck hold."

– from Hunter S. Thompson's column in the June 30 *S.F. Examiner.*

MY FRIEND Hunter has been on a tear lately, and I fear some of his descriptions of events lean towards the apocryphal. Such as the above excerpt from his account of last Thursday's lavish proceedings at Burbank's plush Sheraton-Premier Hotel, site of the tenth annual Erotic Film Awards sponsored by the Adult Film Association of America. I feel one or two minor corrections are in order.

Now, it's true that over 500 people showed for the black tie affair, and true, too, that it cost a C-note to get into the main room where one could rub whatevers with dozens of spiffy sex starlets. And it's also true that the Mitchell brothers, who invited me along at their expense, were the only people to host a lavish private party in a hospitality suite. But, hey, let's set the record straight:

I rarely drink gin. And there are no balconies at the Sheraton-Premier. And no police. Come to think of it, there was no shower stall in the bathroom of our hospitality lounge, which was on the fourth floor. As for the neck hold, that lithe arm around my neck belonged to my dear friend, Seka, the ash-blond superstar who at that moment was whispering to me some small confidence. All I remember is the heat of her breath in my ear.

No, I think maybe Hunter had the wrong guy. Considering he once admitted to having three close personal friends named Jones, he may have experienced a momentary, chemically induced reality shift. It's a nasty business, but these things happen.

Actually, for me the "Smut Awards" were a rather staid affair slightly less important than the fact that I was given an expense paid 24-hour luxury vacation in the Southland. Which is to say, early last Thursday I left dirty dishes in the sink, stepped over a pile of laundry, turned my back on my compost toilet and never looked back.

By mid-morning I was drinking Bloody Marys aboard a PSA flight carrying the Mitchell brothers and an entourage of 28. At Burbank airport we were met by four stretch limousines which whisked us to this magnificent 20-story glass hotel overlooking Universal City.

Once ensconced in my 14th floor suite, I of course called all my Tinsel Town friends to say hello, then put on trunks and headed for the hotel's beautiful garden pool. There an attendant showed me to a chaise lounge and spread on it a fluffy towel bigger than a bedspread. I spent the next three hours chatting with members of our gang, soaking up the sun, cooling off in the pool, and acquiring an amiable buzz from multiple servings of strawberry margaritas brought to my side by a comely waitress in a pink sundress.

Just sign for anything you want. I'm always amazed how quickly I adjust to the pace and decorum of truly gracious living.

That evening found me in the packed lobby in my black tuxedo, looking traditional except for my O'Neill wetsuit surf-

Hunter S. Thompson at home in Woody Creek, Colorado, having just dispatched with an Italian shotgun a vicious magpie tresspassing at the end of his driveway. His pet peacocks nearby never so much as flinched.

ing booties which I wore instead of ill-fitting patent leather shoes. I met my dinner date, an old flame who had to step around Hustler publisher Larry Flynt in his gold-plated wheel chair to reach my side. TV crews and cameras were everywhere. Here was Hollywood glitz to compare with the real Academy Awards, except there was this funny Let's Pretend undertone throughout the proceedings that had everyone grinning. We all knew we were being naughty and decadent and spoofing the whole idea of awarding ourselves prizes for making sex movies.

Dinner was splendid. The award ceremonies opened with a big dance number with naked ladies and smoke bombs. A 20-piece orchestra vamped through the presentation. Artie Mitchell's girlfriend Missy was one of the presenters and looked spectacular in a gold-lamé see-through body stocking.

In all, a brassy, boisterous evening that was enormous fun. I think those Mitchells may be onto something. As for Hunter, it's always nice to see an old friend.

July 3, 1986

A BOLINAS CONFESSIONAL

I NEVER PLAN to do a Bolinas column. Instead, the town encroaches upon the mind. Its existence, its dance, its anger, its nonsense, its hilarity, its idealism, its enormous creativity, at times overwhelm me. Bolinas and its residents over the years have become part of my consciousness, part of my past, a facet of who I am today.

Everything you ever heard about Bolinas is true. How many communities can say that?

I have never lived in the town, but I have spent many days and nights there. I have partied there, made confessions there, spent crazed nights there, been too high to drive home there, been enlightened and frightened and sometimes dragged kicking and screaming into other people's lives. People whose lives were worth being dragged into, and a few that weren't.

One recent Friday night I went there to do my laundry, fully aware that I would drop in on Smiley's bar and get into a low-key goof. I knew enough to know that I was safe leaving the laundromat during the wash phase. It's only when the dryer stops that unattended garments occasionally become free box discoveries.

That sounds like a dig but it isn't. One has to understand the mind-set of downtown Bolinas. I know mothers who take one look at the weekend night circus on the street and fear for their children's well-being. They have reason to do so. I know adults without children who are intimidated by this same theatre — and I understand that, too.

And then there's Smiley's Schooner Saloon. The trick to going to Smiley's is that you don't just walk into the place. First you walk by it. Sometimes there are obeisances to be made, certain people on the street stage with whom it is salutary to visit, to take time to acknowledge. It's not a matter of intimidation, of running a social guantlet. Rather, it is a secular Stations of the Cross. In essence: What's the hurry? Slow down.

Actually, I'm lying. Were I to walk by my old friend T. Bald Eagle and he were to say, "Hey man, what are you so up tight about?" I would know in an instant that he had me. Street karma, pure and simple.

Communities like Stinson Beach would not be as rich as they are today were there no Bolinas. We need Bolinas. I need Bolinas. A lot of beach people occasionally go to Smiley's and drink and shoot pool and get rowdy and revel in the ambiance of what is clearly one of the great honky tonk oases of funk and fantasy anywhere. It can be exhilarating to enter there, a world where the manifest behavior of those present suggests that things are slightly out of control.

And, good Lord, the talent that resides in Bolinas. It's astounding. Among those who live, or have lived, there in recent years, I think of writers Annie Lamott, Jim Anderson, Charles Fox, Aram Saroyan, Mike and Nancy Samuels, poets Joanne

Kyger, the late Richard Brautigan, Robert Creeley, Bobby Creeley, and Bill Talen. And artists Judy Molyneux and Arthur Okamura. And diverse talents such as philospher/private eye Josiah "Tink" Thompson, wood sculptor Tom D'Onofrio, director/sound-genius Walter Murch, ecologist Burr Heneman, Commonweal's Michael Lerner, musicians Dale Pollisar and David Murray, and lawyer Paul Kayfetz (who, controversial as he is, is one of the premier forensic photographers in the business). These are just a few who come to mind.

No, I have never gotten a fix on Bolinas, and that is as it should be. Feature writers may visit the town and document the saga of the Bolinas wye signs and comment on the community as a last refuge of the '60s. I say let 'em.

But the enduring beauty of the town, with its anger and angst, with its struggle to survive the dark forces, is its immense vitality and, somewhere in the mix, a weird and saving sense of humor.

As I said, I haven't figured it out. But hey, the laundromat is alright.

October 23, 1986

Bolinas from the end of the Seadrift spit.
Oil on canvas by Michael Knowlton.

MANNA FOR THE SOUL

On a recent Sunday morning I walked out of a coffee shop in Lovelock, Nevada, already feeling frisky from a ranch breakfast with fresh orange juice and great coffee, got into Blue and pointed her into the rising sun. It was a crisp clear October day and the brown gray slopes of desert mountains looked spectacular through Suncloud Rose dark glasses. I eased Blue up to a loping 75 mph, a piece of cake for a Ford LTD with 400 recently-tuned horses under the hood.

It was all falling into place. A solo shot to the Nevada high desert, a deliberately planned week's vacation, out here alone on the open road, behind the wheel of some of Detroit's best iron, a powerful October sun burning through ice-blue sky, and, good Lord, the breathtaking, awe-inspiring vistas that spread wide and distant with each endless mile.

I let Blue creep up to 80, adjusted the ventilation, and then popped into the cassette deck a tape of Huey Lewis and the

News' LP "Sports." The heartbeat intro to "The Heart of Rock and Roll" came up on the big rear speakers, then the band fired into one of the best kick-ass rock and roll songs of the last decade.

That vast desert kept looking vaster, the road wide and long and holding every promise of adventure, and Huey's music was searing hot, punching out a lilting blues harp solo backed by Johnny Colla's gritty Detroit R&B horn riffs. I felt viseral joy, release, a soaring laughing carefree freedom. No schedule to keep, a few bucks in my pocket, time on my hands, and hauling ass across my favorite desert in the state with the leastest people in the U.S. I kicked Blue up to 90 on a long vacant stretch just for sheer hell of it.

I touched a hundred for a few seconds just to say I'd done it, and let out a howl at the top of my lungs, adding, "Thank you God, goddamn." It simply hardly ever gets any better than that. A fast car, rock and roll, the wide open road, and lookin' for adventure – that's what jazzes me. California born and raised, what can I say.

At such times nothing can really go wrong, even when it does. Four miles east of Carlin (a mobile trailer town of 200 alongside the Western Pacific Railroad tracks), I was holding at 75, thinking about hitting the Commercial Casino in Elko 18 minutes away, when Blue suddenly quit running. As she coasted to a long stop on the side of the road, I felt that sinking feeling. For several long seconds I contemplated the absolute worst that could happen, then shrugged off the fear. Well, kid, here was the adventure you wanted.

I'm no whiz at engines but, by golly, there was the radiator hose leaking steam all over the place, and there was the hole. I walked over to the far side of 80 and within five minutes hitched a ride to Carlin with a deer hunter. Twenty minutes later I'd convinced a high school kid with an earring in one ear to rustle up some duct tape and water and drive me back to the car. He couldn't have been more helpful. Even threw in some antifreeze for me. I paid him $25 and tipped him another five just because the Force was with me, and said much obliged.

Fifty-six minutes after the breakdown I was on the road again, feeling downright spiritual about the whole thing.

I spent the next week in a three-room cabin at 7500 feet in the desert 65 miles north of Elko. The spread belongs to Stinson's Doc Flynn, and he likes having somebody around the place during deer season. For security I had use of a 12-gauge sawed-off semi-automatic shotgun, a Ruger .357 magnum revolver, and, for pack rats (the only critter Doc and I will ever shoot), a .22 LR Walther PPK semi-auto, as nice a piece of machined steel as I've ever seen. You guessed it, I'm a pacifist closet gun freak.

Just as important, I was away from the beach. One has to do that from time to time. To wake up each morning and jog a ways in the silence of the sagebrush, to not hear the ocean, to hear only the ringing in one's ears – that is manna for the soul. Within minutes of the sun breaking over the 11,000-foot peak of snow-covered Jack's Peak, the air would warm to 80. And I'd sit in the kitchen and drink fresh orange juice and feel the warmth of sun on my face, and smell the coffee percolating, and know fully that all I had to do was fire up the 2HP water pump on the creek and maybe catch a trout.

Come nightfall I would listen to the transistor radio, picking up radio mysteries from Canadian stations, and eat a leisurely dinner beneath the light and hiss of the Coleman lamp. And think on things, and sleep long and well. And feel each day the surge of rejuvenation and renewal.

Oh, a few deer hunters came through the property. Couldn't have been nicer. Come to think on it, solo vacations don't come much nicer either.

October 30, 1986

THE FIRES OF WINTER

IT WAS AN HOUR AND A HALF after the sun had dropped below the Farallones, and still it was only 5:30 P.M. Outside a cold wind blustered and postured, blowing every which way like a boxer using fancy footwork before landing the first punch of winter. I knelt before my vintage Bowdoin fireplace, a freestanding hearth with a grate all of 14 inches wide, rather like those small Victorian fireplaces one sees in the book-lined studies of Sherlock Holmes movies. It was time for the daily winter ritual.

One could do worse for ritual than to kneel before the hearth at home. And when I hold a sharp, long-handled axe and bring its blade down on a short length of dry redwood two-by-four, the act itself is a mantra if not a prayer. The sticks of kindling split away with a slight ringing sound as edged steel rhythmically falls along the grain. I take small pride in being able to hold that piece of redwood upright and slice away with no danger to my fingers, like Julia Child chopping celery.

Since the day I moved to the beach, I have been blessed to live in homes with fireplaces. One such abode in which I lived for six years was a large redwood wine vat 18 feet across, up on the Sanford property on Panoramic Highway. You couldn't see it from the road, and friends had difficulty envisioning whether it rested on its side or stood upright on one end. The latter was the case, with a room added on the top end with windows all around. The shingled roof slanted down, giving the barrel a cocked hat cockiness.

The heart of that barrel was a Franklin stove with folding doors, and during many a winter day and night it pulsed with the warmth of burning oak and eucalyptus. When the first rains came, the barrel leaked everywhere more than any one place in particular. But soon the thick redwood staves would swell with the moisture and the big downstairs room would stay warm and cozy.

Along about October of each year a truck would dump a cord of wood on the sloping hillside in front of the barrel. And for the next few days I would pick away at the mountain, loading 18-inch logs into a wheelbarrow and carefully stacking them underneath the front porch. It was good physical plodding work, and I loved it. I was engaged in the pure task of primordial man—seeking warmth against the killing cold and wet of winter.

I finished building the fire, lit the paper with a kitchen match, and watched with keen satisfaction as the first wisps of smoke curled outside the hearth, only to duck back inside as the updraft caught. I noted once again how a cross-hatch of kindling accelerates the burning, insuring a fire hot enough to guarantee the cut-off ends of Douglas fir two-by-fours to get rolling.

A blast of wind threw a handful of raindrops against the window as the fire crackled and hissed. Soon now the first big winter storm should roll through West Marin, and freight train ocean waves will sweep across the sands of Stinson Beach, casting onto the dunes driftwood of all shapes and sizes. A few days of sunshine will dry the flotsam. And then it will be time for me to become the Sunset Beachcomber, ambling among the leviathan logs of winter that have drifted down from the great rivers of the north. I will stuff my gunny sack with food for the hearth. And like an unseasonable Santa Claus in mufti I will carry the sack over my shoulder, my gaze now turned skyward to see the gulls soaring along on the crests of blustery winds, looking quite serious, even as I suspect their secret purpose is nothing other than serious play.

In this season of winter, it is good indeed to spend time before the crackle and hiss and warmth of a well-tended fire.

December 18, 1986

DUMPING WITH DIGNITY

THIS PAST SUNDAY I borrowed a pick-up truck to haul a load of trash to the dump in Point Reyes Station. To some this task may seem utterly mundane; however, for students of dumpology a visit to West Marin Sanitary Landfill can be a rich experience indeed. Perhaps pungent is a better word.

We are fortunate to have here in the west county a world-class dump, one which has been owned for generations by the Martinelli family. The patriarch of the clan, Elmer Martinelli, who is in his 80s now, set the tone, and son Leroy has carried on the tradition, preserving the character of the place.

Years ago, before my first visit there, I sensed greatness when I noticed an ad for the business in this paper, accompanied by the motto, "Dump with dignity." That phrase came to mind as I slowly made my way up the winding dirt road to the current disposal site half way up the hillside. A woman named Wendy, wearing boots and jeans, and a Levi jacket on which were pinned several service medals (quality trash trove) was running the show in between reading a thick hardcover novel. It was a beautiful clear morning, but when I asked, "How ya doin'?" Wendy scowled.

"I'm irritated," she answered, casting a practiced eye over my cargo. "That fellow there who came in before you was lecturing me about world ecology and glacial meltdowns and toxic waste and practically blaming me personally for all of it. Can you believe it? That'll be eight dollars."

I sympathized with Wendy and cheerfully forked over eight bucks. I knew enough not to question her assessment since the large hand-lettered sign behind her read, "Complaining about prices to the person on duty doesn't help."

I backed up next to a row of recently arrived refuse, put on my gloves, and spent the next few minutes off-loading my junk on top of a large pile of ripe cracked-crab remains from a Petaluma Rotary picnic. Returning to the shack and Wendy, I swept out the bed of the truck with a sawed-off broom she was kind enough to offer me from a barrel filled with found brooms and rakes.

"Yup," she said. "I've worked here long enough so I don't smell the dump, but I sure smelled that crab when they drove up with it."

I understood her point and remarked that it was too bad that the customer who had upset her obviously did not understand the true significance of a good country dump.

More's the pity he didn't. Probably a sign of a deprived childhood. How well I remember those occasions when my father would take me to the San Rafael dump on a summer Saturday afternoon. My eyes would bug out looking at mountains of discarded bicycles, radios, TVs, old office machines, appliances and all manner of neat gadgets just waiting for a youngster to rescue. That dump was just possibly the most interesting place I could imagine back then.

Then dad really got me going when he said some day we ought to go there and bring our .22 rifles and shoot big ol' rats that come out around sunset. We never did actually get around to doing that (turned out neither of us was much into shooting animals), but just the thought of a sunset safari at the dump became in itself a cherished father-and-son childhood memory.

"Lot of critters come around here after dark?" I asked.

"You bet," she answered, casting a watchful eye on a young couple wrestling an old refrigerator down off their Datsun pickup. "One time Leroy shot 28 skunks here in one night. They'd overrun the place. And there are I don't know how many feral cats that have dens right in that clump of shrubs up there on the hill. And raccoons and deer and . . . can you see that thing way up on top of the hill there sitting on a rock?"

I followed her gaze and saw what appeared to be a dog or bobcat way up on the horizon. "That's an eagle, I suspect," Wendy explained. "Got a few of 'em around here."

I thanked her for the loan of the broom and drove slowly

out the meandering dirt road, trying to comprehend what insanity must descend upon West Marin Landfill each evening when the sun goes down. Must be a regular critter shoot-out every night. Come to think on it, Mr. Eagle up there looked fat and sassy. I'll bet he had his eye on those crabs.

January 22, 1987

STORM RUN

IT REALLY BEGAN TO POUR as I parked the car at the end of Calle del Sierra. Seeing the beach — angry surf roaring over a blustery on-shore wind, wet sand assaulted by buckshot rain — I almost cancelled. But then I knew this may be the last storm of winter, my last chance to run barefoot in a hard rain, sweating and soaked to the bone, teeth bared to the furies, turning a 30-minute jog into an epic struggle, fighting a good, clean metaphor.

Kicking off my flip-flops I pulled the hood of my sweatshirt over my baseball cap and tied the drawstrings tightly under my chin. And hit it.

The first four minutes were freezing and hard. After that I was thoroughly soaked but warm. And unleashed on a vast wet canvas that belonged to me alone. What'll it be this time? I asked myself. Guilt over having smoked cigarettes last night? Remorse over having offended a friend by something I failed to say? A brutal assessment of career progress? Pick a card.

I realize it's odd that anyone would dwell on any of the above in the midst of glorious nature. But I don't really. The trick is to acknowledge lightly whatever is on the mind, then dedicate the run to renewal. This way every slogging step, every footprint in wet sand, every heave of chest and protest of leg counts as an increment of victory. I can storm against the storm, rage against wind and wild rain. And feel terrific at the end.

My little mind game may be weird, but it gets me out there and running. . . . And besides, it's nice for a change to engage dilemmas of self-knowledge on a dumb physical plane.

This time in the storm, however, I didn't pick a card. Instead I slogged along, a solitary figure moving through the rain, taking it slow and steady. And I thought of the flight of the Voyager, that flying gas tank that accomplished a marvelous feat by going low and slow non-stop around the world. Fact is, going low and slow was the only way they made it.

These days I can really appreciate that. As I reached the beginning of the beach by Seadrift, the storm was lashing my face, pummeling me with 20-mph headwinds. And I thought of how, after finishing my last book in 1982, I had vowed to myself that I would not write another non-fiction book until I had taken the plunge into fiction and either failed or succeeded.

I thought, too, about the three long years that followed during which I was scared to damn death to look at that first blank piece of paper, knowing all the while that I couldn't live with myself if I didn't give it a shot. Then, sometime last summer I found myself holding in my hands the first couple of pages. It was a small quiet start. Nothing to throw a party for. But it was a start. Slow and low.

I seem to recall the folks aboard the Voyager saying the hardest part of the flight was just getting airborne.

Half way up Seadrift I noticed several large pieces of a wrecked boat, probably a fishing vessel, scattered along the riprap. Casualties of the storm. I looked down just in time to avoid stepping on a chunk of decking from which protruded several rusty nails. It took a minute for me to return to my rhythm.

A little further up the beach I reached the orca weather vane by the Allen house and turned back. And thought about one of my favorite aphorisms: the journey is the destination. And realized how hard it has been for me to embrace that truth. Yet, I am fortunate to at least have come to understand better a corollary: that a journey of a thousand miles begins with the first page.

Somehow during the personally stormy months of 1986, the pages kept coming, and I gradually began to feel more like the little engine that could. No heroics. Just low and slow, aided by friends who provided essential mid-course corrections.

Somewhere on the last leg of my run that day in the rain I realized a couple of things: that, no matter what happens (or doesn't happen) to the pages I have written, the Fear is gone. And that the last storm of a long and difficult winter was now behind me.

March 19, 1987

Photo: Michael Sykes.

GETTING TO HUEY

LOOK, IT'S REALLY IMPORTANT," said the editor of *Image* magazine. "We've been trying for months to line up an interview with Huey Lewis. Letters to his manager. Polite phone calls. We've gotten nowhere. Zip. Nada."

"Yeah, isn't that a kick?" I replied. "The guy's such a monster act. Used to live in West Marin. I love it."

"But you mentioned once that you knew him?"

"Yes, but only casually. We chat a bit when we run into each other at parties now and then. See, 10 years ago he picked me up hitchhiking over the hill, and I had my blues harp, and before he dropped me off at the 2 AM Club, he played some killer riffs and . . ."

"Then you can get to him," she interrupted impatiently.

"I could write him."

"You could also speak to him personally at a party."

"What? And blow the guy's privacy? He'd never talk to me again, and I wouldn't blame him. A letter's better. It preserves a certain necessary distance and shows respect."

The editor grudgingly agreed and a few days later I wrote a note to Huey mentioning the magazine's interest and closed by saying if the band was ever up for a story, I'd like a shot at writing it.

A week later I was in Los Angeles visiting some friends who happened to be in the music business and over dinner jokingly referred to the incident with the magazine editor. Whereupon my hosts replied that they knew of publishers and songwriters and musicians who were likewise intent on somehow getting to Huey. It seemed to be Topic A.

These seekers, my friends explained, had gone so far as to visit the 2 AM Club (where the cover photo for the "Sports" LP was taken) in hopes of ever so discreetly running into their man, or one of the members of the band. Others had carefully courted friends of the Star, only to discover that said friends were loathe to intercede on their behalf on any matter to do with business. I understood why, and that gave me an idea.

Shortly after returning home my editor called asking if I had received an answer to my letter. "No," I said, adding that I didn't phrase my query in such a way as to ask for an answer.

"But hang on," I said before she could continue. "I got a much better idea. I'll do a story titled 'Getting to Huey' in which I talk to everyone around him."

I went on to explain Topic A and all the action surrounding the quest, and how it would give me a chance to profile other members of the News in the process, making for a stronger story – ". . . and did you know Huey's sax player Johnny Colla is a killer pool player," blah, blah.

"It wouldn't work," she declared. "It would only show that the magazine doesn't have the clout to get a personal interview with Huey."

I let it go.

Selling snappy story ideas to magazines is very iffy. A few years back, after Israeli jets bombed the Iraqi nuclear reactor, I proposed to *Playboy* a feature on America's fighter pilots, especially the hot shots that attended a combat school called Top Gun. Naww, they said.

A couple of weeks after my last conversation with the editor, I was jogging alone on a foggy deserted Stinson Beach, thinking about my bank balance and wondering if maybe I should have been a bit more forceful in pursuing Huey. I was passing Calle del Embarcadero when I heard my name called.

I looked up and saw in the misty distance a man a woman and a dog. The guy had a baby on his shoulders. I waved hi and continued jogging. But he called a second time and waved me to come over.

Right. Huey, wife Sidney, the kid and the dog, out for a stroll. We chatted for a few minutes, and I found myself being so concerned that he have the beach to himself that I probably seemed a trifle anxious to leave them alone. But Huey, perfectly relaxed, mentioned he got my letter.

At which point I told him about my "Getting to Huey" story, and we both agreed that that was a much better idea, especially since now I had this clever ending in which the writer bumps into his subject by chance and out of respect for privacy and friendship, doesn't ask for an interview.

The next day I fired off a letter to my editor pitching the story again, this time with the true-life twist ending.

I called her a few days later. She said Naww.

June 4, 1987

FELONY FISHING

ONE EVENING a few weeks back, my friend and neighbor Don Beacock phoned to invite me to go salmon fishing the next morning. I leapt at the chance since I hadn't gone out all season. I remember thinking after his call that I had neglected to buy a 1987 fishing license ($10). Not to worry, I told myself. We'll be launching from Seadrift and heading seven miles straight out to the salmon fleet around "C" buoy. The odds have to be one in a thousand we'd ever run into a Fish & Game patrol boat. Heh, heh.

So there we are at 11 the following morning aboard Don's cushy Boston Whaler, feeling terribly pleased to have three nice Coho salmon in the box, when this unmarked fishing skiff with two men aboard cruises up.

Don and I figured the guy in aviator dark glasses and green parka wanted to ask us if we had any luck. Instead he flashes a huge gold badge, announces he's with you know who, and orders us to pull in our starboard lines and prepare to be boarded.

Busted. Popped. Caught in the act. So much for one in a thousand. My heart sank. Visions of hundreds of dollars in fines loomed large in my mind.

Now, I will say that Warden Cole, a square-jawed Sergeant Preston type in his early 40s, was a decent fellow, albeit humorless. Our voices ringing with masterful sincerity, Don and I pleaded our ignorance — or at least our uncertainty — about regulations requiring the use of barbless hooks for salmon and the necessity of clipping off part of a tail fin as soon as a fish is caught. You've never heard a writer and a real estate consultant act more dumb and naïve than we did, our comments heavily laced with, "Golly gee's," and "Is that a fact, officer?"

Warden Cole was unmoved, citing Don for the barbed hooks and no clipped tails. Ditto me, plus a third big one—no license.

"Be prepared to pay some stiff fines, John. Those Fish and Game guys play it strictly by the book," advised big Chris Knowles, a Bolinas commercial fisherman who works at the Stinson Chevron Station in the off season. I believed him. So did Don.

Which was why this past Monday morning we appeared at our arraignments in the Municipal Court (criminal division) of Judge Earnest Zunino. My plan was to play it straight, plead guilty on all counts, and throw myself on the mercy of the court, explaining my behavior as a crime of passion.

For his part, Don confided that actually he knew Zunino from the latter's days as a county prosecutor, but he wasn't counting on any slack. I mentioned that it probably wouldn't help either that I'd just been invited to a cocktail party fundraiser for fellow Muni Judge Lynn O'Mally Taylor.

It was nearly two hours before Judge Zunino got to our cases, two hours of watching a parade of unfortunates (some of them chained and handcuffed) arrested for driving under the influence, drunk driving, battery, possession of cocaine, and similar offenses. I was very impressed with his fairness and patience. The man really took his time with each accused.

I was a trifle nervous when the judge got around to the half dozen Fish and Game cases, especially since he'd dispensed jail time and stiff fines to two dozen defendants who had pled guilty. But as soon as the first guilty sport fisherman (a chemical engineer) took the stand with a fairly outrageous fishing story, things lightened up. After listening to three inventive tales, Judge Zunino grinned and said, "I'm waiting to hear a new story. If I hear one I'll dismiss the charges."

Apparently no one even came close. Fines averaged $100. I was briefly worried when, during his appearance, Don politely pointed out that he had been erroneously cited for improperly fishing for sturgeon, not salmon. Zunino grinned and said, "Very good, Mr. Beacock. I'll dismiss the charge." And fined him a total of $75 for the remaining two counts. When my turn came the judge dropped two of my charges but hit me for $85 for no license. I breathed a sigh of relief.

In all, a cheap price to pay for a quick education in criminal justice. And at least Warden Cole let us keep our fish.

November 19, 1987

RISK TAKING, THANKS GIVING

AIR CRACKLING CLEAR. Scattered cumulus beyond the Farallones. Sand cold and soft to bare feet as I begin my run on the near-empty beach. I'll make this one a solid 45 minutes for a change. I need a long, hard run. Need to blow off tension.

"Hi, John. It's Molly . . . ahh . . . Give me a call when you get in," the message on the PhoneMate requested. Her tone of voice said it all. My call back merely confirmed it: after the first round of submissions New York had rejected my book proposal. Another risk taken. Another failure.

I look out to sea. There is a gap of blue horizon beneath the cloud bank out there. Looks like the sun is going to dazzle the beach with a goodbye kiss. I'm perspiring now. The crisp air feels good.

The book proposal and sample chapters were 177 pages, the product of seven months work with an esteemed woman co-author who has worked every bit as hard. We think it's an intriguing idea for the '80s: a collection of honest, often bawdy, sexual confessions. The first time we submitted the package my agent rejected it. We went back to work and completely rewrote it. Risk taking.

I pass the house with the orca weathervane. A nice rhythm now, a good sweat. The sand soft and cool. And here comes the sun, splashing everything with buttery gold. Blue sky and green hills, damp and lush from yesterday's rain. Crack of waves on wet sand, carpets of abalone-pink foam slide beneath my feet.

Some interesting artistic risks taken these past 18 months. Let's see, two screen plays. Hollywood said, "Thanks, Dude, but no thanks, unless you come down here and do lunch." A large chunk of a historical novel. New York said, "Nice try, but no." And now two strike outs in this go-round.

Funny, the first two rejects felt like a fist in the gut. The third felt like a sucker punch to the kidneys. But the fourth and most recent one was just a glancing blow. Seems easier to get up off the floor.

I pause at the end of the 'drift and drink in the sun, breathe the air, and smile at the heart of sky, the blaze of red and gold. Thanksgiving coming up. Good friends and turkey. Friend Don Leary is hosting a gathering of old friends. It'll be wonderful to see everyone.

A nice rhythm to the home stretch now. On a whim I veer from soft sand to the wet apron of surf, running ankle deep in the caress of the Pacific. The water is surprisingly warm. I playfully splash and kick, feeling the wetness on my legs and face.

I feel giddiness in my chest. It blossoms into a grin. There's the question again: How does it feel to fail? Not once but three and four times? For the first time I hear myself answer: Not bad, actually. Fact is it's a damn sight easier than living too afraid to take the risk at all.

I've done that, too. That really got to me, to know there's something deep within that needs to be answered, to know of an untested creative yearning—and not take the risk. Oh yes, that is far, far worse.

What's this? Two hours since the dreaded news from the Big Apple, and I'm racing through Pacific foam, grinning like a Cheshire cat, feeling the wind, feeling muscles sing? And looking forward to a long hot shower and perhaps a hot brandy and a good book before the fire tonight? I suspect Failure went west with the sun.

To have one's health and perhaps a handle on one's life, to have friends and good will and a clean shot at the brass ring in this wonderous West Marin land—to have these things is a blessing indeed.

Tomorrow I'll throw myself once more into the breech, but

in the meantime, I thank the Almighty for my blessings and pass the gravy. And happy turkey to you, dear reader.

November 25, 1987

INCIDENT ON A WINTER'S NIGHT

WHAT'S THIS TALK about the burned-out road house being haunted?" my friend Walter asked one recent evening at the Sand Dollar. Walter, who moved here two years ago, was referring to the old Over The Hill Bar & Grill just north of Stinson Beach.

"Could be more than talk," I replied, explaining the place has a history of things unexplained and sinister, including a black presence so unspeakably evil that people have fled the premises in terror.

"Some call the place the Black Angel," I added. "Others say 'it' caused the shotgun suicide of one of the bar's previous owners. A priest once performed a formal exorcism, but some locals swear the thing is still there."

"Really?" Walter said, brightening. "Hey, let's go over there and take a quick look."

For some moments I demurred, unwilling to abandon the warmth of the fireside. But finally I agreed, perhaps because I have chronicled the history of the building and felt I might be useful as a guide. Moreover, as a connoisseur of edgework, I found the adventure not without appeal.

We hopped in Walter's black Porsche Targa and a moment later pulled alongside the blackened, silent building. Flashlight in hand, I escorted Walter around the perimeter, explaining the place was boarded and secured. At that point we came upon the main doors – a foot ajar. "Funny," Walter mused, "I had a feeling they'd be open."

Beach town night scene: the Bungalow before it was transformed into the Stinson Beach Grill. Oil on canvas by Michael Knowlton.

"I'll follow you in," I said, handing him my flashlight. "Just be sure nothing else follows you out."

Our inspection tour was without incident. At the conclusion, we returned to the Sand Dollar's warm fireside where the conversation turned to other subjects. This was Tuesday evening.

Thursday morning Walter called from work in Sausalito. His voice was a little shaky. A few moments later I understood why.

"Last night about 1:30 A.M. I was awakened by a voice muttering outside the sliding glass door leading to the deck," he said. (Walter lives on the ground floor of a house on the dunes, and the deck is a foot above the sand.) "I leapt out of bed and saw this figure in black step off the deck onto the sand and move toward the beach. Sliding open the door I said loudly, 'Hey! What are you doing here? Who are you?' But the figure just ignored me.

"I hoped it was only someone harmlessly drunk or stoned but I felt something very strange. I quickly pulled on a t-shirt and sweat pants, grabbed my .25 caliber automatic, and walked out with my dog, a feisty miniature greyhound. The full moon was up, and I could see clearly, but when I got to the edge of the dunes the beach was deserted except for this black blanket lying on the sand about 50 feet away. As I approached, I felt this powerful negative vibe coming from it. My dog's hair stood up and she was growling in a way I've never heard before.

"It seemed impossible there could be anyone under that blanket but when I was a mere 20 feet away suddenly this figure dressed all in black shot straight up from the blanket's center. The face was pale, but I couldn't make out its features. My fear was almost overwhelming. I pulled out my gun and held it in a two-handed combat grip, aiming it at its head. 'Who are you?' I yelled. 'What are you doing here? What do you want?'

"Then the figure turned slowly sideways, looked skyward and raised its arms and let out this long blood-curdling cry. That did it. My dog and I turned and ran back to the house. I was pretty shook up."

Walter was silent a moment. Then, "You think it has anything to do with our going in there the other night? And why did I have the feeling we'd find the front doors open? And come to think of it, why were they open?"

"I dunno, Walter," I answered truthfully. "I really don't know."

January 14, 1988

HOW I MADE PEACE WITH TELEVISION

MAYBE IT WAS THE THUNDER of angry surf in the distance of last night's darkness. Or the howl of wind and the stampede of rain on the roof of the cabin. Or it may have been nothing more than the reflection of firelight off the blank screen of the 19-inch TV screen in the corner. Whatever the cause, something was coming to a head.

For the past three months I have had in my home — for the first time in 14 years — a television set. Doing so was an experiment. A friend had loaned me his old VCR, and I thought it would be great to watch movies from time to time. There were plenty for me to see since, for the past decade, I've gone to about one movie a year.

The two machines were large old clunkers, but they worked. I even rustled up some plywood and paint and with the help of friend Michael Garsva and his table saw, measured and built a nice cabinet that fits perfectly in the corner. When I put the TV and the VCR in there and stood back to admire the results, by golly, I felt like a now kind of guy.

Granted, in the back of my mind lurked a small fear that I might be subtly seduced into spending hours each day before the screen. I had read somewhere that in the average American household the TV is turned on an astounding 7½ hours a day.

I needn't have worried, having in three months tuned in only '49ers games and a few KQED specials. As for videos, they were all right for awhile. However, I confess 90 percent of the much-touted movies I rented were disappointments. And watching two features at one sitting left me numb and feeling I'd wasted several hours. Gradually, I began to resent not so much television (which is a terrific medium) but what had become of it.

Last night as I sat before the fire, and under the influence of nothing more than the two glasses of Chianti I imbibed with dinner, my resentment blossomed into a grand annoyance with the TV set itself.

That old Sylvania, even when turned off and blank, seemed no less an intrusion than when turned on. The machine had become for me a symbol of mass market mediocrity, a spewing standpipe of low-brow entertainment shot through with the commercial hyperbole of turd merchants. Making matters worse, the use of the TV and the VCR had become a source of tension in a much-valued relationship.

The latter realization was the last straw. I sensed the onset of a fine madness. Yet before gathering rage tempted me to commit a hasty, regrettable – nay, irrational – act, higher instincts prevailed. A vision of ritual expiation and glorious riddance came to mind.

Abandoning my seat before the hearth, I pulled on my waders, shrugged into my foul weather jacket and, with a certain rough relish, pulled that 40-pound lower chakra mind-magnet from its corner perch. Outside, the storm raged as I dumped the set into the trunk of my car and headed for my destination.

The waves were huge, and the on-shore gale force wind screamed as I strode purposefully onto a deserted portion of the beach, lugging the set into the heart of a nasty night. Wading out in the swirling foam, I dropped the TV into shallow water and stepped back a few paces. Seconds before a large incoming wall of white water engulfed the machine, I aimed a Colt .45 caliber revolver at the screen and fired five shots. The tube imploded with a noise I can only describe as thoroughly satisfying. I stood there in the storm and roared with laughter, feeling very much at peace.

Yes, I shot my television. Flat out drilled the sucker. Truthfully, in retrospect my one concern was I might be littering the beach, which, as you know, is against the law. Thus, early this morning I returned and found the demolished set some distance from the point of its demise and removed it for proper disposal.

Oh, and just now I put on the shelf of the corner cabinet my collection of books by Joseph Conrad and Arthur Conan Doyle. They look wonderful.

January 21, 1988

THOSE INNOCENT ICE PICKS

IT HAPPENED one recent afternoon during a small barbecue birthday party. I was reminiscing with a friend, whom I'd first met during my late-blooming hippie days, and mentioned the eventful months in 1971 when I had lived in the large Mill Valley household of DJ Big Daddy Tom Donahue, who pioneered FM underground radio. At that moment a woman who was listening spoke.

"Yeah," she quipped. "I heard you were really unbearable."

I looked at her and smiled, trying to maintain composure while I removed the ice pick from my stomach. There was no blood, but the pain was no less visceral.

Looking at her, I saw no hint of malice in her eyes. She was smiling, seemingly unaware of the small devastation she had wrought. I grinned gamely and replied breezily, "Yeah, I'm sure I was." And began to say something when she interrupted.

"A lot of people still think you are, but I tell them, 'No, he's not really. I know him. He's okay.'"

It wasn't an ice pick I was feeling. It was a knife blade embedded to the hilt and now being twisted. My feelings recoiled, withering to smoked ashes like the crushed legs of the witch in the *Wizard of Oz*. Devastated, I mumbled some lame reply and excused myself to help grill hamburgers on the Weber outside.

It was a few minutes before I regained composure, aided by a gut feeling that the woman, whom I consider a friend, was entirely ignorant of the disruption she had caused. Perhaps I should have later drawn her aside and mentioned the episode, but that afternoon I was in no mood to instruct anybody about anything.

Perhaps, too, it's not a good idea to appear in the society of others when one's self esteem is a sheet of thin ice melting in the springtime sun over a lake seething with demons. We all have days like that, times when we're not just running on Empty. We're running on Reserve. Sometimes we're not truly aware just how vulnerable we are to the knives and ice picks that fly about the arena of society, whether hurled by chance or intention.

"The definition of manners," Emily Post explained, "is behavior based on a natural sensitivity and awareness of the pain of others." I wish years ago I had been made to understand the profound usefulness of her pronouncement, for perhaps I would have avoided those awful occasions when I have blurted out those innocent but hurtful words that I later learn have cut someone to the quick. Yes, unbearable indeed.

Of late I have found it helpful to be a bit more courtly in my behavior to others, as though they were privately running on Reserve. I have discovered that, literally, it doesn't hurt.

Of course, it's a lot easier to have a thick skin when one is feeling on top of the world. And who doesn't appreciate hearing a withering riposte when delivered by such legends as writer Dorothy Parker, who elevated the put-down to high art. Still, I don't think I'd want to make a career out of such civilized skewering.

Then, too, there are times when the quip is clearly unintentional, hurts like hell, but you have to laugh. For instance, years ago I was sitting at the bar in the Sand Dollar with a fellow Stinson Beach resident when the woman next to him struck up a conversation with him. She was quite tipsy but amiable, and as my friend got up to leave she said with complete sincerity,

"Listen, I know how people in this town feel about you, but I really think you're nice."

My friend, with astounding aplomb, thanked her and gave her a hug. Outside we laughed. But oh, the pain. I can still feel the memory of it.

Sensitive? Yes, I confess it. But aren't we all? We live in small communities in West Marin, villages comprised of small social groups and extended families. It can be wonderful but the risk one takes in becoming involved, becoming visible, is that from time to time one takes a few shots to one's ego, to one's self esteem, to one's heart.

Sure, it's worth it, but in the meantime, let's hear it for good manners. Please.

April 21, 1988

RESPITE IN THE WATER

IT WAS A CUMULATIVE HUNGER that had been building for months, a need to be among them, perhaps in some small way to be a part of them. They were out there. On calm mornings when the sun shot up over the mountain and washed the bay and the village in gold, I watched them. And on days when thick fog rolled in from ambush to muffle the shoreline, I had walked on wet sand, watching for signs of their arrival.

Even at night—especially at night—I could hear them moving on to the shore, announcing their presence with a series of unsyncopated "whumps," and hisses, and sighs. Here and there a sharp "crack" would accent their uncadenced surf beat. Can there be a more efficacious lure to the arms of Morpheus than their muted siren call?

Yes, I was starved for a wave — any wave. I had not been in the water for months, really been in it, head over heels, floating and splashing and playing and dancing with water in motion. And for this lover of the ocean, that just ain't natural.

So the other morning I solemnly put everything else in life on hold and took myself to Kirby Ferris's Live Water Surf Shop (wonderful name for a surf shop) and rented a pair of Churchill fins and a Boogie Board.

Down on the beach at the end of Calle del Sierra I struggled into my faded O'Neill "Animal Skin" wetsuit, donned the fins, and plunged happily into the surf. As I kick-paddled my way through a tame shorebreak on the foam belly board, an incoming hedgerow of white water rolled over me, slapping me in the face. The chill water was electrifying. Rivulets of water trickled here and there into my wetsuit. I shook my head and blinked the salt water out of my eyes and continued paddling. Further out, just beyond the break zone, I floated in the undulating furrows of watery crest and trough. Howdy, ocean.

As usual I was once more reminded how simple a thing it is to get in the water, how wonderful the experience, and how dumb I am not to get out there at least once or twice a week, regardless of the weather and conditions.

Imagine being able to slip on a wetsuit of thin neoprene rubber (for some of my friends, this alone would be pretty hot stuff) and to jump into the cold waters of the Pacific and yet feel absolutely toasty. As the folks at O'Neill like to say, "It's always summer on the inside." And then, picture yourself floating in a state of near neutral bouyancy bordering on weightlessness, just outside the surf zone, and experiencing the rush of a moving wall of tons of water sucking you into its embrace, lifting you up its face, then passing beneath you as you slide down into the trough. For a second or two your view of the shore is blocked by the back of that wave as you hear it explode onto shallow water.

For this wipeout artist, it's still a thrill every time — one which I doubt I'll ever outgrow — even as I continue to discover new meanings in my dance with one of the oldest forms in nature.

And it is a dance. Whether I surf a wave (even badly, which is most of the time) or merely float up and over its liquid contours, I feel I am dancing intimately with something powerful, something untamed, pure and in perfect harmony with creation.

I suspect the joy and release and just plain fun I experience in such moments derives from the harmony of that dance. Then, too, when one is constantly moving in and on water, swimming and kicking and holding one's breath, and plotting moves, the rest of the workaday cares of the world disappear. Ah yes, respite in thc water.

There are myriad ways in which to find such respite. But there's something about the ocean, even about its seeming total indifference to man, to its own beauty and power, that for me will remain a lifelong fascination.

For the better part of an hour I reveled alone in the surf, stalking the larger waves and sliding down and across their short-lived breaking walls, happily letting them mug me with exploding white water, feeling at peace and very much alive.

And that is a very nice feeling indeed.

May 26, 1988

The famous (now defunct) Michael Roach Band. Left to right: Mike Love, Clay Lilleston, John Ridella, Roger Chrissinger, Mike Lowry and Michael Roach. In its day, a fine rockabilly bar band.

MY NIGHT AS A DOORMAN

JOHN," SAID MICHAEL LOVE, a member of the Michael Roach Band, "how'd you like to work the door for us when we play the Bolinas Community Center Saturday night?"

"Sounds okay to me," I replied, feeling mellow from my Vedanta retreat this past Memorial Day. "I just take their money and stamp their hands, right?" "That's about it," Mike replied, looking somewhere over my shoulder.

And so I blithely showed up this past Saturday night at the Bolinas Community Center at 8:30 P.M. and helped set up. I pulled a long folding table into place near the side door, helped adjust the lights, set up a cash drawer and broke a $20 bill at The

Shop to provide ticket change. Over in one corner two people from *The Hearsay News* sat behind a beer and wine concession to benefit the paper. Prior to the start I wrote down two names for the band's guest list. This should be a piece of cake, I thought.

It was nearly 9:30 when the band kicked off the show, and right away some one on the band's guest list entered accompanied by a lady friend she insisted be admitted without popping $4. I declined and was treated to sincere invective, this as a small crowd of hyperactive, skateboard carrying semi-to-full-bore latch-key teens crowded the foyer peeking and bobbing and using the restrooms.

I sensed immediately I would need help to physically restrain incoming cattle. Fortunately Paul Guerin volunteered. His help came not a minute too soon, for there began a parade of folks who insisted they didn't have to pay, this for an astounding number of reasons: "What'd 'ya mean I'm not on the guest list. There's gotta be a mistake." "I'm friends of the band." "Let me in and I'll check with the piano player." "I'm here to sit in." "I'm working the house lights." "I'm looking for my kid." "I don't have any money." "I'm the sound man." "I'm director of the Community Center." And, "Hey, man, you know me. I'm your friend."

Real trouble came when a troupe of editors of *The Hearsay News* arrived to run the beer concession. Not having been instructed as to how these things work, I momentarily stalled their advance, thereby setting off esteemed poet Joanne Kyger whom I've long considered a friend. She was outraged, incensed, livid.

The band got louder, and so did the cattle, and so did I, losing friends and making enemies as fast as I took in money. "Look!" I shouted again and again. "Pay the four bucks and if the band okays you, I'll reimburse you, no big deal!"

It was a big deal. I looked at my watch. My god, only an hour had passed. A second wave assaulted the door, headed by the Rossi brothers, two young handsome up-and-coming BoBo musicians carrying guitar cases and accompanied by assorted girlfriends and hangers-on. They were playing during intermission, they insisted. I knew from nothing and held firm.

Jostling and shouting and angry cries. A beer bottle broke

on the floor, and from nowhere a man saying he was the janitor demanded entry. How inventive, I thought. (Turns out he *was* the janitor.) Just then the aforementioned livid Joanne Kyger grabbed the ticket table and angrily dragged it out onto the dance floor, shouting, "This is Bolinas! Let the people in! Fill this place! You're the worst, the toughest door man I've ever seen! You're just into making money!"

"Dammit! Joanne. I'm working for free!" I yelled back, lunging for the table and pulling it back into place. Two other women came up and demanded I lower the price, shouting, "This is Bolinas, people have no money!" Another helpfully offered to take over the door while I took a break. More shouting and yelling and argument. More latch-keyers gawking and weaving, dogs and little children wandering in and out. Noise, chaos, shouts and heavy negative vibes.

At 11 P.M. and exhausted, I gave up and let everyone in for free. I went backstage and tallied up the sales. About 60 paid admissions – a light turn-out. But the lesson was clear: no matter how fond I am of Bolinas, working the door at BoBo on a Saturday night is one of the most brutal, thankless jobs in all of rock and roll.

June 9, 1988

OUR LITTLE TOWN

STINSON BEACH looked nice and Christmasy this past weekend, and the splendid weather attracted lots of visitors. While they soaked up the sun and country-village ambience, other events were occurring around them.

Shortly after dinner Friday a motorist reported a pick-up truck on fire on Shoreline Highway near Red Rock Beach. Fire Chief Kendrick Rand paged out for a crew and within minutes a pumper rolled to the scene. We arrived to find a truck completely engulfed in a tower of flame and smoke.

Greg Shirfey, Pat Norton and Terry Swift quickly deployed a hose and attacked the fire, being careful to avoid toxic-laden smoke and remaining at a safe distance in case the gas tank exploded. Car fires are always dangerous. Car fires at night on the cliffs of Shoreline Highway with no occupant present are also suspicious. We looked over the cliff with flashlights.

Moments later a Sheriff's deputy rushed to the scene and with uncommon speed radioed in the license plate number for an ID. He explained there had been a reported truck sighting in the county involving the kidnapped 9-year-old girl Michaela Garecht. False alarm. Our little town.

Saturday morning the volunteers strung Christmas tree lights on the fire house and fir tree next to the Barn downtown. Coffee and rolls were served. People on horseback ambled by. We talked about the upcoming annual firemen's dinner that evening. Our little town.

Just before dusk a call came in that a young man was stuck on a tiny ledge 100 feet up a cliff at Steep Ravine beach. Within half an hour, an eight-man crew of Stinson firefighters, assisted by State and Park Rangers, reached a spot 170 feet above the man. Using National Park Service climbing gear, the team quickly rigged for a cliff rescue, and in pitch-black darkness lowered big Terry Swift down a vertical face while 27 stories below him the surf pounded the rocks.

Terry, wearing a miner's head lamp, had to pendulum over to reach the frightened man, tie him into a second rope, then assist him as the two were lowered 100 feet to the beach. They had 30 feet of rope to spare. It was a tricky, difficult, nervy and dangerous night time cliff rescue that prevented a tragedy. Our little town.

Because of the rescue the firemen's annual dinner started a little late. In a generous gesture Tom and Karen Horton, who own the Stinson Beach Grill (closed for the holidays), donated the use of the restaurant for the occasion. It was a fine evening and the department's sense of pride and achievement and cohesiveness was downright palpable.

Sunday morning our ambulance responded to "a man

down" in a ditch and transported him to the hospital.

By mid-afternoon the sunny patio of the Sand Dollar was packed with brunch-time patrons when we learned a sports car had plunged into the lagoon two miles north. Firefighters arrived to find a telephone pole snapped off at the base and pieces of a car's body scattered about, but no car, and no driver. Fearing the worst, Kendrick ordered a Coast Guard helicopter scrambled. The atmosphere was tense. Jeffrey Trotter quickly donned a wet suit and dove in to search for the car. A moment later Pat Norton, using scuba gear and fins, began an underwater search pattern in the 15-foot-deep channel.

Twenty minutes later the driver, a man in his twenties, arrived with his parents to say he'd escaped unhurt from the late model Corvette and that there had been no passengers. The chopper, already airborne, was cancelled. Our little town.

It was close to 5 P.M. when the call came in that a cyclist in Seadrift had fallen and sustained a possibly serious head injury. As the volunteer ambulance rolled by the Sand Dollar, the patio was still crowded. Our little town.

December 8, 1988

FLOATING ISLAND

THE OTHER AFTERNOON I drove to Point Reyes Station to pick up a bit of typesetting I had ordered from my friend Michael Sykes. His Archetype West is a busy little enterprise located in a couple of rooms on top of the Old Western Saloon. And since I'd be seeing him at the end of business hours, I brought along a promising-looking bottle of '81 Anderson Valley Cabernet on the off chance we'd be sharing a glass or two.

I wasn't disappointed. Fact is, Michael's semi-occasional end-of-the-day wine and cheese gatherings are a kind of west county ritual on these cold winter afternoons. And because his Floating Island press is considered one of the premier small presses in the country, as often as not a poet or writer from around the Bay Area will drop by.

Today it was a fellow in cowboy boots, Levis and a jean jacket stretched out on the couch in the production room across the hall from the office where Michael works on his Compugraphic typesetting machine. Poet Stephan Torre bestirred himself and apologized from succumbing to a nap attack induced by a glass of excellent Zinfandel. He is a clear-eyed intelligent man who looks in his early forties, lives mostly on Inverness Ridge, dividing the rest of his time between Berkeley and a small ranch he owns in British Columbia.

"Oh my, an '81," Michael said as I handed him my offering. As he disappeared into the bathroom across the hall to rinse out a couple of wine glasses, Stephan somehow coaxed me to read him a prosaic page or two from a work in progress.

"Can't get much of a handle on your writing from that," he said sociably. "But that description of the gold-leaf, filigreed book lettering. Now, you might hang on that one awhile when you rewrite."

And off we went — chatting about writing and books and small presses while from out of Michael's office wafted music from Dylan's LP "Biograph." The long narrow room in which we sat is remarkable. There's the comfortable funky sofa and

Michael Sykes, publisher, poet, and man of serious high whimsy.

several chairs, between which is a fifties-style coffee table covered with wine glasses, cheese, crackers and copies of poetry monthlies and earnest-looking chapbooks seething with passion and difficult truth.

Surrounding this arrangement are walls of books, wonderful old books, wonderful new books — an ancient text on alchemy by Johannes Fabricus, poetry by Robert Bly, Bill Witherup, and Stinson's Gino Sky, old hardbound volumes by Joyce, Hemingway, and Joan Didion. And on the brown sandblasted tongue-and-groove walls are framed photos of people and scenes by Inverness photographer Thomas Weir, posters from art museums with vivid color reproductions of Edward Hopper's works and posters announcing exhibitions of Dürer woodcuts and engravings.

There are Oaxacan rugs on the floor, hand-painted Mexican folk art bark paintings tacked on the wall, a wine rack, small shelves with sea shells, bric-a-brac — wonderful comfortable warm collected clutter.

And joining us now was poet Brent Reiten and a lovely dark-eyed young woman he introduced as Toni. Next came Inverness artist Cyndie Huegel celebrating the publication of a physiology textbook containing her exacting medical sketches. "My specialty is brains and guts," she said cheerily, offering a delicious salmon pâté she'd just bought from the Palace Market.

Michael joined us now, followed soon thereafter by his longtime paramour Cindy Ohama. More chairs were provided. Wonderful wine, wonderful conversation, great people and chit chat and laughter and books and so much warmth. Here was vintage Berkeley without Berkeley's hassles. And who could have minded the occasional strains of Patsy Cline from the juke box downstairs?

Michael Sykes, man of letters, man of serious high whimsy, has indeed created a floating island where kindred spirits may celebrate their deep affection for this gentle shared ritual and the miracle of the written word exquisitely printed. Thanks, amigo. We are all grateful.

February 16, 1989

THE GREAT GADGET REVOLT

I'M NOT SURE, but it may havc had something to do with the recent cold snap. Or the ghastly way my portable radio met its end. But something set them off—at least enough of them to qualify as a mutiny.

It was probably the portable radio. One evening as I was doing the dishes, the radio, which was perched precariously on the shelf above the sink, fell and hit the edge of the plastic dish pan. I managed to grab it just as one corner dipped into the water. Worried that the thing would short circuit when I switched from batteries to a wall plug, I put it in the oven and turned the thermostat up to 200 degrees to gently dry any moisture from the internal wiring.

And promptly forgot all about it until I was about to turn in. Opening the oven, I saw the radio lying on its side, its horribly warped plastic case looking like it had been through a two-hour taffy pull. I shrugged and unceremoniously chucked the carcass into the garbage and went to bed.

I awoke about 3 A.M. to the sound of my Thrifty Drug bedside electric alarm clock grinding its plastic gears. Sleepily I turned the clock on its side, hoping that gravity would reduce gear friction. It didn't. I pulled the plug and went back to sleep, only to be awakened again, this time by the low hum of the toaster oven turning on. Leaping out of bed and freezing in the night, I observed that I'd neglected to turn the toaster thermostat dial all the way down. I pulled the plug irritably and returned to bed.

Outside the arctic wind blew, turning my new revolving ventilator cap on the chimney this way and that as it was designed to do. Only at 4:30 A.M. the device began acting like it had no lubrication. Down the chimney and into the fireplace at the foot of my bed came horrible amplified screeches and scrapings. No chorus of rutting felines or the death squeals of roof rats impaled on the fangs of raccoons could equal this eerie howl of tortured tin. Burying my head beneath the pillows, I fought for sleep shuddering at the thought that these were the unanswered cries a dying radio would make upon the untended altar of cremation.

At daybreak I discovered my troubles were not over. Indeed, the mutiny spread. During important business calls my phone would go dead. This because the little plastic connector to the base of the phone wiggled loose from its contacts. A felt-tip pen inexplicably leaked all over the front of my favorite purple shirt. The answering machine deleted the beep at the end of my outgoing message. What a chicken move!

"Look!" I shouted to the empty cabin. "I'm sorry about frying the portable! Okay? I miss it, too!" I had to get out of there.

That morning on the way to Point Reyes Station in Big Blue, the FM portion of the dash radio went out, followed by zero audio when I tried to play a cassette. Oh no, they must have gotten a message through. Afraid to think about the implications, I drove on in silence, now turning on the car heater.

No heat, or darn little. Oh no! Et tu, Blue?

Later, in my hillside writing studio, when my computer began acting strangely, I closed up shop for the day and sought refuge in The Gym where I told my story to John "Rocky" Ballouz, the gym's genial bearded proprietor and computer whiz. John, who understands many things, nodded sagely.

"That's exactly what happened," he said. "Gadgets from time to time will gang up on you. I've seen it happen. They play hard ball. You let one or two of them step out of line and start calling the shots, and they take over. Don't ever let them possess you. You did right to walk out. They'll get the message."

A moment later I used John's phone to call my answering machine. At the end of my outgoing message I heard the beep. I couldn't help smiling. The revolt was over. The gadgets got the message. And so had I.

February 23, 1989

DINNER FOR THE ALUMS

LOOKING AROUND the dining room of the Parkside Cafe on this memorable evening, I counted 31 of us gathered here for this first ever get-together. Thirty-one Stinson Beach residents ranging in age from mid-twenties to mid-seventies. Some of us had lived here since the late Pleistocene; others had arrived only a few years back.

We were a diverse lot: bartenders, waitresses, music teachers, housewives, Grateful Dead staffers, park rangers, restaurant owners and managers, realtors, poets, sales reps, mechanics, carpenters, bakers, rock 'n roll techies, landscape contractors, computer nerds, secretaries, paramedics, stationary engineers, and even a writer or two. Small towns being what they are, there was probably no love lost between some of us, but any fussing and feuding was put aside for the night, for we were here to celebrate.

We gathered to pay tribute to something larger than we were, something to which over the years we had all contributed, something about which we were very proud, namely the oldest, continuing, most dedicated, on-call, 24-hours-a-day, come-as-you-are, get-'em-to-the-doc-on-time, don't-worry-be-snappy, rural, volunteer fire department ambulance corp in the whole damn state of California.

Truth to tell, the rest of the Stinson Beach volunteer fire department was with us in spirit this evening, for without them the medical end of rescue work would simply not be possible. But on this occasion the people the department especially wished to honor were the Stinson Beach pioneers who nearly two decades ago had the gumption and dedication to create a badly needed volunteer ambulance service — and who manned the thing night and day, sometimes on a wing and a prayer. Ye Gods, to think that the village once got by with only a used station wagon and a couple of dog-eared, Red Cross first-aid books.

Some of the alumni have moved away or passed on, but close to a dozen were on hand (characters, every one of 'em). And they shared with us incomparable war stories from the early years that were powerful and moving, and often hilarious. Mostly the latter, for it is in the nature of the human spirit to find respite in black humor when faced with sometimes horrible suffering.

To hear Marna Griffin, this elegant, stately, gracious woman, who once headed the corps, describing in dulcet tones how she once rode to the hospital in the back of the ambulance attending a huge gorilla of an LSD-crazed bodybuilder who threatened to tear people's heads off (while others in the ambulance cowered in terror), was priceless. And that was just for openers.

There was no shortage of stories, not with people with jobs and families who, when the fire phone rings, drop everything

The 1988 joint muster and barbeque of the Stinson Beach and Bolinas volunteer fire departments at Audubon Canyon Ranch. Another great portrait opportunity for distinguished photographer Art Rogers.

and rush to help. Not with people who leap out of bed in the middle of the night and within minutes, to cite just one example, are risking their lives on the side of a cliff in the rain doing CPR to a bloody, dying fall victim while a roaring Coast Guard chopper hovers overhead.

Why do they volunteer? There are a lot of secondary reasons. Some, like me, love trouble like an old fire horse. Others, like Jeffrey Trotter, remember the expression of profound relief on the face of the wounded, fallen young climber who had already survived two days in a rock crevice just above the surf and who faced certain death from exposure if not found soon – "the look on his face more than paid for all my months of training." It is indeed fulfilling to be able to help save lives.

But I suspect the primary reason why they (like those before them) volunteer is because in this small community, in this dynamic maturing democracy that is America, the unselfish lending of a hand to one's brothers and sisters is simply the decent thing to do. And that is, after all, a big reason why we're all here in the first place.

March 2, 1989

STORM SURFER

THE WAVES near the lagoon entrance at the northern end of the beach were a jumble of gray, shifting, four-foot peaks beneath dark clouds and rain. No one was out, but he didn't care. He preferred being alone this time. He needed to be in the water, needed to punch through the shorebreak, take off and get creamed a few times. For the first 15 minutes he worked himself hard, paddling with intensity, working off the adrenaline, giving his muscles a work-out, grabbing any wave that promised a decent drop and a quick rush.

He was riding his seven-six tri-fin, good for late take-offs and fast tight cutbacks on walls that closed out quickly—as these were doing. Twice he made suicide back-door drops, jammed to the bottom into the collapsing power pocket, and deliberately ate it, letting his body relax as he was rolled and pummeled by exploding water.

He spotted a chunky, jagged five-foot wall moving in from outside and sprinted the distance just in time to spin around and stroke into it. The surface of the breaking wave was layered with four-inch chop and his board chattered loudly as he shot down the face, struggling to keep from spinning out. The drop was exhilarating. Using the speed picked up from a carving bottom turn, he angled up the wall and kicked out onto the back side an instant before the wave sectioned. He paddled out just beyond the break zone and paused several minutes for a breather.

He sat up astride his board and peeled back the neoprene cuff of his right wrist to look at his dive watch. 6:13 P.M.—close to slack high tide. There would be little or no longshore current to carry him out of position. He pulled his wetsuit hood back off his head and looked around. As incoming waves lifted him to their crests he saw the beachfront houses through the mist and rain, saw carpets of white water rushing up the wet beach to lap at the low dunes. Rain pelted his face and he raised his head and stuck out his tongue for a taste of sweetwater.

He looked seaward, feeling the warm moist wind. This was the kind of storm he loved—subtropical, wet, blustery, and fast-moving with pulses of fat rain, almost like monsoon showers. He turned shoreward again and saw on the steep hills behind the village vagrant puffs of cloud grazing along the tops of the pine and redwood trees while in the gusty air around him he smelled chimney smoke from the homes along the dunes. The smoke was tinged with the sweet pungency of creosote released from the driftwood logs which fueled many a beach hearth during cold winter days.

A thick gray wall of water swept him up its side and onto its feathering crest. The silent languorous power of the wave, mere seconds away from exploding, infused him with a deep, resonant feeling of well-being. As he floated down the steep backside into the trough, the horizon disappeared. The wave broke with the muffled roar of water colliding with water.

He felt a warmth spreading through his stomach, as though he had just downed a shot of superior brandy. No, these waves weren't much for surf. They were unpredictable, peaky, gnarly, and covered with chop — he judged wave texture like grades of sandpaper with these being about a 36 grit — but he rejoiced to be among them. True, they were mere elements of nature in motion, unconscious and indifferent to his presence. At times they terrified him, even attempted to kill him. Certainly they never showed him favor. Instead they made him earn everything he ever got from them.

He knew his casual regard for them as animated things was baseless anthropomorphic projection. And yet from his earliest days in the ocean it had been natural for him to give them attributes of sentience and heart, for so often these same waves had nourished him, healed him, scolded him, provided refuge, cradled him, taught him, thrilled him — even on rare occasions carried him to a transcendent realm. And for these things Dana Kidd loved waves; he loved them with all his heart.

(Excerpted from a work in progress.)

March 16, 1989

Storm swell: local kahuna (and Live Water Surf Shop owner) Kirby Ferris at a West Marin secret spot tapping the juice of a clean winter wall. Photo: Fred Murtz.

HIGHWAY I TRAFFIC SOLUTION

I HAVE FOLLOWED with interest CalTrans' plans to straighten and widen Highway 1 here and there in West Marin, making it easier for traffic to speed around curves. Perhaps this is intended to mitigate some of the traffic jams created by CalTrans' recent double striping of all but 246 yards of this scenic road, thereby increasing the driving stress level in the west county by a factor of three while lowering the safety level by nearly the same amount.

Now, if I correctly understand these CalTrans chaps, they had to double stripe in order to qualify for federal funds amounting to 85 percent of the money needed for make-work projects to solve the problem caused by double striping. Right . . .

Nevertheless, an indignant West Marin is united in its opposition to this plan. Elsewhere, this weekly has suggested that more turnouts be created.

This idea has some merit, but I submit there may be a more satisfying solution: rather than mess with the highway, CalTrans should install car blasters on every vehicle whose owner has lived more than three years in West Marin.

This sensible alternative occurred to me the other afternoon as I was stuck on Shoreline Highway behind a white, four-door sedan, on the rear bumper of which was a sticker with the dreaded words, Alamo Car Rentals. The vehicle was, predictably, moving at 22.5 mph, its driver failing to take any notice of the turnouts, let alone his rear-view mirror.

It would have been wonderful to press a button to flip the heads-up display panel into position, watch the Mark IV Top Gun blaster instantly appear on hydraulic risers from its concealed hood compartment, and observe the automatic targeting mechanism position the cross-hairs onto that sedan's trunk compartment. Once I heard the locked-on-target signal tone, I would merely press a second button, and BARROOM! An explosive projectile traveling at twice the speed of sound would explode the sumbitch into biodegradable confetti.

CalTrans might even offer alternative weapons, such as slower heat-seeking, tail-pipe bombs or percussion grenades, the latter designed merely to stun the target into weaving wildly off the road, preferably over the side of a cliff.

Granted, there are minor problems associated with this scenario. Metal confetti is not yet biodegradable. And the noise would disturb wildlife. And rusting dead cars at the bottoms of cliffs are unsightly to hikers and birders. But I'm prepared to live with these while we seek answers.

What about the people in the cars, you ask? What people? These are not real people. Drivers are required by law to be at least marginally conscious, to pull over when five or more cars are behind them, to use turnouts, to avoid driving at dangerously slow speeds, to look in their damn REAR-VIEW MIRRORS!

No, these are not people. Unconscious breathers, maybe. Carbon-based, brain-dead life forms, possibly. But sentient beings with the intelligence of a gerbil? Get serious, Sherlock. How many times have you seen some ratchet-jawed urinal cake at the wheel turn to his seat mate and gesture with his free hand as he slows to 15 mph going into a 30 mph turn? And repeat this for eight twisting miles? Brain dead breathers, the lot of 'em!

Once, during the dotted-line days, I was accelerating to pass one of these creeping cakes on the straight-away by the Olema Cemetery when she suddenly slammed to a halt. I went into a horrifying, screeching four-wheel skid for 60 feet, stopping within ten inches of her rear bumper. Shaken and angry, I confronted the woman and was advised in righteous tones that she had stopped to avoid hitting a quail scampering across the road.

Blasters, CalTrans. And while we're at it, let's get Fish & Game to issue licenses for daytime hunting of Winnebagos.

Thank you, dear reader, for allowing me to contribute some constructive thoughts to this important public debate.

June 22, 1989

FOG MANTRA, FOG LAUGHTER

I WOKE UP at daybreak this morning and saw for the first time in weeks the thick mist of fog swirling about the tops of the pine trees. After weeks of sunshine and high winds, I welcomed the change. Standing outside on my porch, I noted the muffled sound of the waves and knew that the ocean would be flat calm and slate gray, the air above the water cool and still.

I abandoned my usual morning routine of breakfast and a three-minute commute in Blue to my hillside writing studio. Instead, I threw on a pair of sweat pants, a t-shirt and a windbreaker and headed for the beach. I knew I would find the graceful arc of Stinson Beach vast and empty — and I needed that. I needed to go for a long easy run and to be away from people, to jog alone on wet sand and watch the small Pacific waves peel off in precise accordance with the harmony of Nature. Heartbeats of a planet, their soothing cadence was a needed balm.

Half way down Seadrift, I passed a juvenile turkey buzzard picking at the remains of a dead gull. It seemed to sense my indifference for I passed within 20 feet before he bestirred himself and launched into a lazy low circle. I could hear the beating of his wings against the air. A bit further along I passed a dead murre amongst the flotsam of the last high tide. And here and there along the water's edge were stranded jellyfish the size of Frisbees. Nature's casual carnage on the shoreline of a small coastal town, detritus from life's unceasing cycle.

I found a large piece of driftwood at the water's edge and sat there cross-legged, gazing across the slate lake before me, admiring the way the fog just offshore blurred the horizon line. The resulting illusion of infinitude drew my gaze into the heart of the vast Pacific. I sat very still for awhile, thinking about peoples' pain and suffering, about rage, about tangled lives, about choice and responsibility, and about turkey buzzards and jellyfish and, just now, the possible state of mind of the harbor seal peeking out at me from the lip of a breaking wavelet. Funny how life's most profound concerns can be found interwoven with the most petty speculations.

And then I turned around to be sure the coast was clear, turned back to face the ocean, and began chanting a mantra in a loud voice while trying to think about nothing at all.

It is not often that that I run at dawn, or chant on a log, or awaken with a need of the ocean's steadying influence, but on this morning I did. Thus it was a wonder to find an oily Pacific ready to calm the troubled waters of my mind. And calm them it did, for after 15 minutes of chanting and being very serious and dramatic and heavy and a trifle self-conscious, I suddenly burst out laughing—and knew that once more all was right with the world.

What made me laugh? The sudden memory of a classic one-liner. It happened one night when the Stinson Beach Volunteer Fire Department rescued a motorist who had driven off a cliff. Because of the patient's condition, Fire Chief Kendrick Rand ordered a helicopter from Sonoma which soon arrived and made a dramatic flare-lit landing on Shoreline Highway. All told, a dozen emergency vehicles, their red and blue lights flashing, arrived from CHP, National Parks, County paramedics, State Parks, County Fire, and Sheriff. The scene had a very real life and death look.

With commendable speed the rescuers had the patient stabilized and during the 20 minutes it took to carry the fellow up the road there remained little for anyone to do. In the meantime a thick fog swept in from the ocean. So here were all these serious, uniformed paramedics and law enforcement fellows standing around killing time. At that point Kendrick Rand, esteemed Fire Chief and Incident Commander, looked up at me and Michael Perry who were standing on a fire truck holding spotlights, and directed us to lower our light beams a little.

A little puzzled, we did as directed, at which point Kendrick held his two hands up to one side and made shadow puppets against the fog, saying, "Okay, now here's a doggie chasing the bunny. . . ."

July 27, 1989

SUPER GOPHER

THE OTHER SUNNY DAY while sitting quietly high on Inverness Ridge admiring the view of Black Mountain, I heard just behind me a rustle of grass. Looking to its source I saw the head of a furry brown gopher poking out of his burrow to grab the stalk of a nearby wildflower. Cute little critter, I thought to myself. The sight reminded me of a famous gopher story that has become a part of the rich folklore of Stinson Beach.

Some years ago when John and Beth Perry and their two children moved into a rambling comfortable ranch house on the hillside above Stinson Beach, they were delighted with the promise of the place. The house was on a two-acre parcel with plenty of room for a vegetable garden, a lumber shed, and a wood-working shop (John is a fine builder by trade).

There was also an overgrown lawn in front of the house which John mowed with great difficulty, for it was covered with large mounds of dirt, some of them new, some quite ancient. Gophers, John concluded. He made a mental note to pick up a couple of traps at Bolinas nursery, little realizing the strange odyssey on which he was about to embark.

Buying two spring-loaded gopher traps, he carefully set them in the tunnels beneath fresh mounds and began a routine of checking them each evening before dinner. A week passed, and neither trap had been touched. But two new dirt mounds appeared nearby.

Mystified, John turned to local experts. These were both numerous and disposed to preach wildly conflicting theories with a zeal one often associates with memories of a painful past. In the absence of universal wisdom he proceeded with the Boiled Trap Theory whereby all human scent is removed, following which the instruments of death are placed in situ with gloved hands. Another week passed. Nothing. And another dirt mound.

Clearly the traps were being scoffed at by the gopher, for by now the experts agreed this was the work of only one gopher. Moreover, this was no garden variety critter but a rare and remarkable fluke of nature, like a rogue shark, or a killer wave, or a white stag. This was Super Gopher.

"It became a personal thing," John confessed one evening as we sat at his kitchen table drinking beer. "I switched to igniting many sticks of Gopher Gas — at great expense, I might add. The place looked like a Chinese funeral."

New and larger mounds appeared in the days that followed. Steeling his resolve, John obtained a rare copy of a .38 Caliber Exploding Gopher Trap, an ingenious but highly unstable device invented in the 1940s which, when triggered in a tunnel, fires a special cartridge filled with bird shot. John fenced off the lawn to keep out his son Mathew and daughter Annie, ages four and five at the time. As the trap was periodically moved, the boards he laid atop the tunnel entrances for safety were killing the lawn. John shrugged at this disclosure, explaining, "There are some things a man just has to do."

Alas, when the exploding trap drew a blank, John removed it and abandoned the field to his adversary.

Four years passed. Many more dirt mounds appeared. Finally, one warm spring morning Supergopher surfaced and, with daring aplomb, basked in the sun. John, who was sitting in the kitchen with his brother Jim (a Buddhist monk who, parenthetically, is a former fraternity brother of mine from Cal Berkeley) ran for his .22 caliber target pistol. He returned only to discover that brother Jim had rushed out onto the lawn and flapped his robes and shooed the creature back into his lair.

"Supergopher was saved that day by organized religion," John recounted sadly. "For this I cut off part of Jim's rice supply."
Next week: a strange ending.

August 10, 1989

Illustration: Walt Stewart.

SUPER GOPHER'S STRANGE END

LAST WEEK I recounted here the unsuccessful four-year struggle of Stinson Beach homeowner John Perry to eradicate from his lawn an extraordinary gopher whose cunning and resilience had earned it the grudging admiration of the entire village. "All at my own expense," John adds. And now the conclusion of our story:

Several weeks after his brother Jim, a Buddhist monk, had flapped his robes and shooed Super Gopher (who was basking in the sun) back into his hole while John ran for his .22 target pistol, John had another golden opportunity. One sunny morning Super Gopher again appeared at the entrance to his lair and this time, sans monk in the wings, John quietly approached to within three feet of his quarry, triumphantly looked his target dead in the eye down the barrel of his pistol, fired the coup de gras — and missed.

For this the man had to face his children Mathew and Annie literally rolling on the floor laughing at their father. "My wife Beth had merely collapsed laughing onto a kitchen chair."

In the aftermath John toyed with a special weapons approach — for example, an assault rifle that fires hollow point bullets with hot "gopher loads," or a compound hunting bow with exploding tip arrows (rumored to be available on the black market). However, these devices were costly for their intended purpose, dangerous to have around the house, and their use required skill and patience. With manly restraint John settled for more pedestrian approaches such as baiting the gopher traps with gobs of Dolores Cutter's Old Fashioned Crunchy Peanut Butter. But all to no avail.

"In my heart I knew all I was doing was keeping the lawn watered and nicely maintained while he gradually turned it into the Moon."

Then one day after several more months had passed, a strange and wonderful thing happened. A friend, who supplemented his earnings by growing and selling a local variety of cannibis known affectionately as Stinson Blue, happened by and heard of John's plight. Taking pity on his friend, the man offered to bait a trap with a pristine and pungent sensimilla bud that he just happened to have with him. With an indifferent shrug born of years of failed remedies, John agreed, and moments later the trap was baited, set and laid.

In an hour Super Gopher had succumbed.

As John finished the story of his six-year struggle, he took a sip from his can of Pabst Blue Ribbon, then rose from the kitchen table and went to the refrigerator. Opening the freezer compartment he removed a brown paper bag and handed it to me, inviting me to examine its contents. Inside was the body of a large, quite old gopher, one which, even though shriveled and frozen solid, bore in repose the stamp of cunning and greatness.

To my question John replied that famed professional taxidermist Fred Funk, who lived in Stinson Beach at the time, had agreed to render the remains into a trophy rug for the mantle of the Perry's living room fireplace, complete with bared teeth and a velvet backing. John balked at my suggestion that Super Gopher be mounted in a standing position with its head held high in the fashion of a noble stag at sunrise. "I've managed to retire a legend," he explained. "And I want it to look retired." In the meantime, John reported, several of his neighbors who had heard of his success were growing one or two cannibis plants "purely for gopher protection."

He looked once more upon the frozen visage of his old adversary before he closed the paper bag and replaced it in the freezer compartment. Then John resumed his seat at the table, took another sip of beer, and sighed, adding philosophically as he stared into space, "Yeah, ol' Stinson Blue won the big one."

August 17, 1989

THE SECRET OF DILLON BEACH

DID YOU HAPPEN to see the story on Marin in Monday's *Chron*? The report focused on how the state's richest county is succumbing to the crunch of cars and people. Nothing new, except a side bar called "The Secret Charms of Marin County." One of the entries reads: "Everyone knows about Bolinas, which makes a big public fuss about being a secret. But the real insiders head for Dillon Beach, in the far northwestern corner of Marin, where seals often outnumber people."

This was news to me, since the very day before, as a warm blustery subtropical storm rumbled and thundered its way across West Marin, I had invited dear friend Susan for a walk on Dillon Beach. By golly, there's nothing like a bracing stroll along a wave-ravaged shore, followed by an Irish coffee somewhere. Especially for us real insiders.

We hopped in Blue and moseyed up Highway 1, rolling into Dillon Beach a little after 1 P.M. Sure enough, the beach was rainy, deserted and wave-tossed — perfect for an adventurous walk. Matter of fact the whole town looked deserted. I noted with satisfaction that the place didn't look any different than it did that memorable evening a few years back when the citizenry discovered that a stuck toilet had completely drained the town's water supply. A story like that is a country news editor's dream. In fact, writer Dave Mitchell's story in *The Light* about the mishap won him a prestigious award.

I headed for a vacant dirt lot behind the dunes and was about to enter when I noticed a kiosk at the entrance with a sign reading "Parking $3." Could there possibly be someone inside on such a wet, stormy day? There was.

Nonsense, I thought, and looked around for a place to park

alongside the road. Yet all we saw were "No Parking" signs. A couple of hundred yards farther on we came upon the entrance to Lawson's Landing – day use $4 per car.

"Hang on a second," I announced confidently as I pulled up near the ticket booth. "Maybe I can use my *Point Reyes Light* credentials to get us in just to park." After all, I thought, we're insiders. It began to rain as I stood in front of the booth, talking through the opening of a cloudy sliding window at a pleasant woman in her fifties.

"Uh huh," she nodded, smiling as I explained my intimate connection with a Pulitzer Prize-winning periodical. "I just moved here last December. That'll be four dollars."

"Say," I countered in my best folksy manner, "you don't suppose Nancy Volger is in the boat house, do you?" Which was to say, "My close personal friend Nancy about whose resort I have written glowing columns which have, in turn, inspired countless real West Marin insiders to visit Lawson's Landing (at four dollars a car) would certainly be happy to let us in at no charge if she only knew we had arrived and were standing here in the rain."

"She just went home. You wanna call her?"

"Oh, gosh, no," I quickly demurred. "I wouldn't want to disturb her. That's fine."

"Well, then, I guess you'll just have to pay four dollars."

I had to appreciate this woman's professionalism, having myself once spent an eventful evening as a door man in Bolinas for the Michael Roach band.

The rain began falling hard as I climbed back into Blue. Susan smiled as I explained that I was merely hesitating on principal to pay four bucks to walk on a public beach in my own backyard. And when she suggested barbecued oysters at Nick's Cove, I happily pointed Blue toward Tomales Bay.

The oysters were marvelous. So were the Irish coffees. We felt like real insiders.

September 21, 1989

UPROAR IN DILLON BEACH

IT SEEMS MY COLUMN, "The Secret of Dillon Beach," a couple of weeks back kicked over the ant hill up in those parts. You may recall I described driving there one recent rainy Sunday for a walk on an empty beach and discovered to my surprise no place to park Blue without forking over at least three bucks to the folks who own Lawson's Landing and Lawson's Resort. Moreover – and this was the secret – for all practical purposes there is no free public parking anywhere in the town of Dillon Beach.

In other words, there's a fine public beach up there but if you're behind the wheel, you can't get there from here – not for free, anyhow. Which was why I opted instead for oysters at Nick's Cove.

Judging from my mail, it seems the column hit a sore spot. "Mean-spirited," "inappropriate," "condescending," "jeering," and "cynical" wrote Helen and Kent Lawson and Nancy and Bill Vogler, the resorts' owners. They advised that my taxes do not pay for the facilities, restrooms, security, and cleanliness of these privately owned resorts. Gosh, I sure hope not.

Now let me say right here that the Lawsons and the Voglers are fine and generous people. They got a great resort. And when next I go there I'll happily pay the $4 day-use fee. It's a heck of a good deal.

But folks, on that stormy Sunday I didn't want to go to your resort. I didn't want to go anywhere *near* your resort. I didn't want to see anybody. I just wanted to drive to a little cul de sac beach town on the northern California coast and park somewhere and go for a quiet walk on the damn beach – owned by California taxpayers – without having to reach for my wallet.

Evidently, in Dillon Beach, this is asking too much.

The Lawsons and Voglers "wonder if Grissim asked for free oysters and coffee when he stopped at Nick's Cove." Nope, but it didn't cost me three bucks to park, either.

"John, be of good cheer," writes a Dillon Beach resident in a personal letter (I'm withholding her name since I know how things can get out of hand in kicked-over ant hills, not to mention small towns). "I visited Dillon Beach for many years before I moved here and I have yet to figure a way to crack that place sans fee. . . . They (the owners) are good people but their attitude is "Everyone pays". . . . It's mildly frustrating when you would like to show guests the beach. But I balk at paying for what amounts to a drive-through."

Elsewhere, in last week's letters to the Editor, Dillon Beach resident Carol Kaney, referring to the same column, was appalled by my behavior. She was perplexed why the editor continues to let someone of my caliber write for this paper, adding, "This man needs to get a real job instead of spending his time hunting up stories with his girlfriend on some beach sucking oysters."

Now we're getting somewhere.

Ms. Kaney, I couldn't agree with you more. How a prize-winning editor continues to allow a writer of my caliber to write for his weekly while showing no shame at my scandalously low rate of remuneration remains a deep mystery.

As for your other recommendation, great idea. I confess I have never had a real job, and I'm here to tell you that there's a lot to be said about such a thing. The truth is that, while writing can be a great way to make a killing, it's no way to make a living. No, freelance journalism is not all it's cracked up to be. Oh, I know it may sound all right to be on a beach somewhere sucking oysters with my girlfriend, but I must be honest. When I do stuff like that, I assure you, the last thing I'm doing is hunting up stories.

Anyhow, just to keep the facts straight, you might recall I never did spend any time on the beach that day. And it wasn't me, but the parking, that was doing the sucking.

October 5, 1989

QUIET CHANGE

A FEW MOMENTS BEFORE SUNRISE this morning, I sat abed with fingers curled around a mug of hot tea—Russian Caravan steeped four minutes in an infusion ball, then stirred with milk and honey. Comforting early morning rituals. Outside the window at the foot of my bed, a small flock of birds landed on the wires on either side of the telephone pole and began their own daily ritual, preening and stretching and flitting from one wire to the next like dancing musical notes in a Disney cartoon.

I've mentioned these birdie notes a time or two in past columns, which have occupied this corner of page five for close to six years now. I tend to reflect on such statistics around this time, for Thanksgiving week marks the beginning of the holidays, a season I either dread or embrace, depending on how the year has gone—or is going. And, to be honest, for too many years recently, these final weeks of the year have been tough sledding for this would-be Santa Claus.

Looking back, it was in part my longing to remove the dread from the season that led me about a year ago to attempt to make some changes in my life, to shake up the status quo and punch through to . . . something. Precisely what I sought was unknown to me, nor were the means to the end especially apparent. But the hunger was deep, oh so very deep.

I had long known that the early hours of morning have always been a calm and powerful time for me, so I began rising at 5:30 A.M. to read and reflect. To do so meant turning in early, which effectively ended visits to the bar for after-dinner libation. Which in turn led to a total loss of appetite for tobacco and even the occasional use of illicit substances. These things occurred gradually over a period of months. It was not a struggle. There were no chains of addiction to break, just a need for a change. It was a quiet thing, really.

The first hint of change was a growing clarity. Each morning those birds on the wire and the trees and the sunrise became a little bit sharper, their colors more vibrant, the play of light and shadow on the canvas of nature richer. I love that time of morning, a time when the village is silent and empty and at peace. Before long I myself felt the same way, which led to all manner of meditations.

Truly I knew not where I was headed, only that I needed to head there, to break out of the rut I had been in for years, and to make something happen. And happen it has, on many fronts. This spring, with absolutely no warning, I entered into a relationship that has in the most wonderful fashion exploded all my previous conceptions of how powerful such pairings can be.

By the same token, the responsibilities of that relationship have tested me in ways I never envisioned. It is a strange experience indeed for this 18-year bachelor to begin to explore the dark caverns within himself and to shine the light on the fears and weaknesses that dwell therein.

To examine oneself, especially when a caring partner is

helping wield the scalpel and the flashlight, has been at times terrifying. With trembling footsteps I ventured inside and kicked awake a very large dragon of anger that I didn't know lived there and which has never really been asleep. I have made the acquaintance of Monsieur Denial who was attired in all manner of elegant finery and whose speech was most refined and whose arguments were wonderfully convincing and artfully false.

The exploration has been scary and exhilarating and boggling but each time I emerge from those cold icy caves, I feel as though the light of understanding and love has melted yet another block of frozen beliefs, broken loose fear, or triggered another avalanche of old memories and trapped feelings that needed to be felt.

This morning as I sipped my tea and looked at the birds, I thought to myself I still don't know quite how all this will turn out, but my heart was bursting with the spirit of Thanksgiving.

November 22, 1989

THE RAGING COLUMNIST

IT WAS EARLY EVENING when I finally admitted that the dark and decidedly un-Christmasy thoughts about him which had been preoccupying my mind had fanned my brooding anger into rage. And since the latter emotion is a recent and still unfamiliar newcomer to my inner landscape, I was unprepared for its seductive ferocity. I had to do something to ease the pressure, and quickly.

Using a 12-gauge pump shotgun to blow away a wall of shelves filled with Mexican pottery and glass jars sounded like a most satisfying solution, but none of the ingredients were available on short notice. Instead, I put on swim trunks and a t-shirt and hit the beach, reasoning that a long hard run would help reduce rage the same way it had done in the past with depression, grief and fear.

The beach was deserted and magnificent. The air was cold and calm and a nearly full moon hovered over the Pacific, its light reflecting off the glassy slopes of breaking waves, turning the swept clean sand chalk white. Blind to the beauty, I charged the water line with a full head of steam.

I was also blind to the two-foot-high cut in the sand which the afternoon's high tide had carved away from the beach. I went sprawling face down. Unhurt but furious at this latest insult, I clawed myself to my feet and ran toward Seadrift, filled with murderous thoughts.

Quite unexpectedly, about a hundred yards into the run, I started growling in the direction of the surf, as though the object of my rage were there. Then I began woofing, imagining myself in a confrontation, stabbing the air with violent punctuations. This quickly escalated to barking. At first I felt extremely self-conscious, embarrassed to be doing something so silly. This is all well and good for people in therapy with their inflatable Hit-Me, Hug-Me Herbies, I thought. But certainly not me, not this easy-going beach dweller who had merely exhausted his reserves trying to remain civil and avoid expressing overt hostility. But I wasn't hostile. You wanna see HOSTILE? I'LL SHOW YOU HOSTILE! WHY YOU . . . !

And there I was, running along the water's edge shouting epithets and accusations at the top of my voice, now screaming at the ocean, threatening, accusing, swearing, punching the air, abandoning myself to a blood-lust rage, feeling its almost sexual energy course through my veins, fueling the adrenalin rush, pushing me to run harder.

And I did. I ran nearly full tilt for more than 30 minutes, then bolted into the surf and literally punched with my fists several waves as they rolled over me. I hardly felt the icy cold water, but when I raised my voice to yell once more, only a wheezing sound came out. I had shouted myself hoarse. After toweling off, I trudged off the beach, feeling drained, purged of rage, free from the grasp of a dark demon. I remembered Shakespeare's apt description of a kindred passion, jealousy: "That green-eyed monster that doth mock the food on which it feeds." As for the object of my rage, I simply shrugged and thought, "Eh, get a life."

After a hot shower and a light supper, I savored the quiet bliss of being free of the tension and anger that had been plaguing me. The feeling was both somatic and pyschic. It felt grand to be clear — and wonderfully tired. Couldn't keep my eyes open past eight that night.

Funny thing, rage. Like anger, it seems to spring from that fertile ground between desire and fear. Yet unlike anger, which most regard as very unpleasant, rage is a seductive elixir, for it makes one feel impervious to pain, all-powerful, and deliciously just. That's one dangerous mix.

Like a kid who has just learned to ride a bicycle, I'm still getting the hang of it, so if one night you see some weirdo out there swearing at the surf and punching the waves, rest assured he's probably harmless. But just the same, I'll keep an eye on him.

December 14, 1989

KITTY DAY

ACCORDING TO THE LETTER Santa Claus wrote to Susan's five-year-old son Jasen, there was a special kitten waiting just for him at the Humane Society. And today was Kitty Day. So we three bundled into Susan's VW Rabbit and headed for the Society's Novato headquarters.

"We'll call it Bat Kitty," I joked over my shoulder to Jasen as he sat in his car seat with his blanket. His love of Batman toys and clothes had recently prompted me to dub him Bat Baby.

"No. I'll name it Sara," Bat Baby retorted breezily, then returned to sucking his thumb.

Fine with me, I thought to myself. This should be like a quick trip to the pound — look over a cage full of fur balls, pick one out, plunk down a few bucks for shots, and be out in a few minutes.

Half an hour later, as we pulled up to the posh entrance of what appeared to be either the Hyatt Lake Tahoe or the Bear Valley Visitors Center, replete with a large Bufano statue of a bear nursing two cubs, something told me the Marin County Humane Society might be a tad different than the Biloxi, Mississippi, animal shelter.

Sure enough, we entered a spacious, airy world of pleasant staff aided by confident Junior League volunteers in Levis and Harris tweed sport coats with patched elbows. Judging from the memorial plaques everywhere, half the rich deceased LOLs in Marin County left it all to Poopsie and the Humane Society.

The lady behind the desk gave Bat Baby a balloon while Susan submitted to a 20-minute interview about her fitness for kitty ownership.

Impatient with all this frou-frou rigamarole I was about to say, "Chrissake, lady, we're not here for a bank loan, just a goddamn cat for a kid! Be grateful we're saving it from the gas chamber!" But at that instant the interview ended. A matronly volunteer ushered us into a room full of stainless steel cages, only three of which had cats. Right, cats don't have litters in winter, suggesting to me there are more homeless hungry people in Marin County these days than there are pets in like circumstance.

Fortunately, one of the three cats was a cuddly eight-month-old black Siamese female named Felicity. Her computer-generated profile sheet claimed she is gentle and friendly and will make a wonderful house cat. We took her. Thirty minutes and $72 later we were on our way home with Felicity, now meowing loudly in the back seat, inside a cardboard box with air holes.

"Kalisha!" Bat Baby suddenly proclaimed, looking at the box next to him. "Her name is Kalisha." Susan and I grinned at each other and shrugged. And at the very word the cat howled ominously and clawed at her confines with increasing ferocity.

By the time we reached Mountain Home Inn cute little Kalisha had become something from Night of the Living Dead. Amidst hideous sounds of animal rage and the tearing of cardboard, the box rocked back and forth on the seat. Bat Baby grew increasingly anxious, as did his mom who reached back to hold the box upright. More ripping of cardboard as an air hole grew larger. Suddenly a claw shot out in front of Bat Baby's face. Trapped in his car seat, he threw his head back and yelled bloody murder. The car was now filled with screams and tearing and clawing and meowing and panicked Bat Babies and frantic moms.

"My God!" Susan cried. "It's getting out! Pull over!" I did so and only just managed to turn around in time to grab the monster by the throat as it lurched through the hole it had torn open. I pushed it back inside and pressed an address book across the opening. Susan took the wheel while I tried to keep a lid on both the box and my laughter.

That night Kalisha slept at the end of Bat Baby's bed, perfectly at home with her new friend. We've all taken quite a shine to her.

January 18, 1990

TYPEWRITER MEMORIES

ONE AFTERNOON a few weeks ago I walked on Stinson Beach at low tide and after a moment's study, made an X in the sand. I then returned to a large driftwood log by the dunes on which I had placed an old Underwood manual office typewriter. Leaning on the log next to it were a shovel and a hoe.

"I've found just the spot for you," I said to her in my mind, grasping the machine by the cross bar with the tab settings and hefting it on to my left hip. With the digging tools in my other hand, I trudged the 50-yard distance back to the X in the sand.

As I slowly, methodically began digging a hole, I thought back on the 15 years I had been with this old girl, of the thousands of hours I had spent with her, of the joy and anguish I had known. And the grinding work, and boredom, and the many times I just sat there looking at a blank piece of paper rolled onto her carriage waiting, hoping, and occasionally praying.

The sand was damp but not wet as I roughed out a two-foot diameter hole with the shovel and began digging for depth. The work went easily. Truth to tell, I had spent more time in the presence of that machine during that period of my life than I had with any other machine, automobile, residence, or relationship.

No, I didn't have a name for her, but the very day I picked her out at the Typewriter Kings in San Rafael (she got her start in the *IJ* newsroom, a good omen), she felt like a she. Not a vamp or a mistress or a fickle girl, but a good woman, rock steady (she weighed 28 pounds) and reliable. I only had to have her cleaned once and get the "w" fixed. She was always there for me, and never acted up on those mornings when I didn't especially want to go to her. And because of that loyalty, I was honoring her by a decent burial by my beloved Pacific Ocean.

Once before, in 1974, I had performed this same ritual, burying in the dunes by Jose Patio a trusty Royal that had seen me through two books and a broken heart. The Rowan Brothers, Chris and Lorin, and Chris' then-girlfriend Betsy, assisted with that candlelighted dusk internment. Betsy played the flute and the brothers serenaded with guitars. Two days later I left on a 15-month round-the-world odyssey. Typewriter memories.

The hole was at least three feet deep now. I switched to the hoe and used its squared edge to carve and shape the sides of the grave into a square. As I did I wondered if Ms. Underwood felt any resentment that I had kept her around for a few years after I got my computer. Or that I had eventually moved her out onto the porch to fend off attacks of snails and sleepless rust, not to mention an exploratory tendril from the blackberry bush.

A young couple stopped to politely inquire what I was doing. I answered but when they asked what I wrote, I demurred, explaining the hour at hand belonged to my typewriter, not me. They beamed New Age smiles and nodded and thanked me for sharing. And, come to think on it, left rather quickly.

The hole was ready now, its bottom a good four feet deep. I lifted the old girl and gingerly lowered her down, feeling a pang of guilt as I noticed the rust and corrosion on her frame. At least

I hadn't abandoned her to the rummage sale, I reassured myself. As I tossed the first shovel full of sand on her, I felt a certain writerly sadness.

Three days ago, on the morning following last week's storms and high surf, Ms. Underwood mysteriously reappeared, perched jauntily atop the same large driftwood log by the dunes. Probably some passerby had put her there after the storm waves had pulled off the sandy overburden. She had been scoured clean of rust and sparkled in the sun. I got the message and apologized, and promised her the full WD-40 treatment when I once again laid her in her sarcophagus of sand.

After all, the woman likes to look her best.

January 25, 1990

Ah, the late-seventies look. The vintage Underwood was as much mistress as machine. Photo: Shirley Sanford.

THE BARREL IN THE MIST

IT WAS STILL QUITE EARLY this morning when I neared my studio up on the north forty. Just short of my destination I pulled into the front yard of Jack and Wendy Hunt's house to feed their critters, something I'd agreed to do while they were away a few days. I parked in the front yard and stepped out — and into a reverie.

The landscape about me was cloaked in a thick, warm mist, utterly silent except for the low, throaty neighing of the horses in the corral. The yard, which had pleasantly gone to seed, was lush with the wetness of last night's surprise rain. Here and there patches of knee-high grass were bowed over, heavy with shimmering droplets. Next to the wet woodpile the sprawling echium bush was a freeze-frame explosion of tendrils tipped with long cones of bright blue blossoms, each of which held a tiny droplet of water just waiting for the merest touch to be released.

In the distance, barely visible in the thick mist, was the outline of the converted wine vat in which during the seventies I had lived for five years and two books. Ah, the wine barrel, once a vision of hipness for a young writer, scene of sunny quiet mornings and after-hours parties, of laughter and women and drugs and Steely Dan at full volume, an abode ideal for cultivating the image of the colorful adventurer and beach bachelor who smoked Shermans and wrote for *Rolling Stone* and who talked of having a visiting Julie Christie up for tea. And who said nothing at all about the dark nights of his impoverished soul (and matching bank balance), of the sometimes terrible aloneness, and the Fear. Oh, what a time it was.

I glanced down and saw among the weeds a robust carpet of purple and white African daisies that I planted six years ago.

The wine vat came from Ukiah, was 19 feet in diameter, drafty in summer, leaky in winter, hard to heat, and the most wonderful place a struggling writer could possibly hope to live. Photo taken from a magazine about weird houses. Photographer unknown.

By then I had moved out of the barrel, but I occasionally did gardening here for the previous owner Shirley Sanford. I remembered saying how much I had enjoyed the task, which was less than half true, for I refused to admit to myself that I found the work galling. Why? Because I was doing the gardening in trade, being unable to pay Shirley $50 a month for the rent of a shed out back which I used for a studio.

Had I been working productively or striving to meet prudent financial objectives—had I had a clear plan of any kind—my gardening exchange would have been a wonderful short-term arrangement. But I hadn't. Instead I had let my career stagnate in a West Marin lotus land, and as often as not the monthly $50 I could have scraped together went up my nose. And so I planted daisies and smiled and tried to ignore that I was on my knees, tried to deny the tin taste of failure and bitter self-loathing, the sudden full memory of which I now felt in the pit of my stomach.

An impatient neigh interrupted my thoughts, and I set about my chores, feeding the horses, letting out Mr. Goose and four ducks, and filling the cat bowls with kibble. As I topped off the corral water trough with a hose, I glanced once again at the echium bush, marveling at how spectacular it was, then remembered that I myself had planted it years ago, having discovered it as a small volunteer among the African daisies.

My chores finished, I stepped over to the bush for a closer examination of the tiny water drops in the blossoms. They seemed to be little pearls waiting to fall on some fortunate passerby, chance gifts in the form of epiphanies of sudden understanding. Then, too, the echium plant itself was a stately thing, slowly grown through tough seasons to wisdom and fullness.

I took a last slow look at the yard and the rampant garden in which I had once labored with hidden bitterness, and realized that there had been a fair bit of growth since then. Turning to leave, my shoulder lightly brushed the echium.

April 26, 1990

CAMPING WITH AMERICA

THE CAMPSITE WE FOUND last Monday afternoon was perfect — nestled in lodgepole pines next to a brook. The ground around the fire pit and picnic table was strangely wet, but we were enchanted.

With pioneer gusto, I assembled the dome tent while Susan fired up the Coleman stove and her five-year-old son Jasen, whom I've dubbed Bat Baby, happily scurried about. We savored a fried chicken dinner and the balmy high Sierra weather and turned in at dark. We never heard the bear that raided the adjacent campsite.

No, the first sign of the problem appeared at mid-morning the next day when a crush of people appeared at the small lush pond in which we were swimming and sunning. By noon the place was inundated — and loud. Two women appeared and without a word took over half of our picnic table. When a school bus appeared through the pines to disgorge a load of day campers, we fled.

Back at our camp, we watched in amazement as our babbling brook overflowed its banks within a half hour period, threatening to flood us out. Turns out a vigorous family of beavers in the area have been damming major streams at night, causing severe fluctuations during the day.

We moved camp to a new site nearby, finishing just as a large and loud family of what appeared to be blue collar Native American Indians from the Reno area moved in just across the narrow asphalt lane that weaves through the campgrounds. By dusk the happy campers had built a huge bonfire and were shouting and yelling and laughing. The cacophony continued until around midnight, punctuated now and then by a young man in his late twenties, bare-chested and wearing dark glasses, beer in hand, pacing the perimeter of the fire slapping his belly and chanting, "Hey-ya ai-ya hay-ay ai-ya," in some vaguely menacing declaration of manhood.

Following a fitful night's sleep, we awoke to find more RVs had arrived while Bat Baby began throwing up. We spent the day nursing the little guy through his tummy flu, noting that the campgrounds during the day were largely vacant and quiet. Our brief respite ended that evening, interrupted this time not by our Reno neighbors but by an even more terrible scourge.

Lying in our tent shortly after 9 P.M., we heard in the near distance a horrible screeching scraping sound, as though a bulldozer were dragging through the campgrounds on its side the wreckage of a Winnebago totalled by a head-on collision with a logging truck. As the shrieking, 110-decibel sound grew near, Bat Baby shouted questions. I hastily pulled on my jeans, grabbed a flashlight, and rushed angrily to the narrow road to confront the roaring beast.

The horrible screeching sound was upon me as my flashlight's beam penetrated the darkness ahead, revealing nothing. It was only when I lowered it that I saw a little girl about eight astride a set of Big Wheels, one of those all-plastic tricycles with a big wheel and high handles and a little low seat. Incredibly, the hollow plastic wheels grinding against the gravel and asphalt of the campsite road were responsible for the deafening racket.

Dumbly staring at me as I spoke in a trembling voice, the child reversed her course, but not before Susan and I had to disperse a dozen or so children attracted by the tumult who came running through our campsite.

Thursday morning our Reno neighbors departed, leaving several burnt steaks and packets of lunchmeat perched on fire logs to attract bears. Next to us a couple with three out-of-control children and a boom box playing heavy metal rock took up residence. Like the rest of the American citizenry who had come here, they had brought it all with them.

Faced with a Friday night arrival crunch, we opted to end our adventure a day early. Still, it was worth it. This was Bat Baby's first camping trip, first time in a rowboat, and first trout caught. He had a terrific time.

July 26, 1990

THE COMMANDER CHECKS IN

GEORGE FRAYNE, aka Commander Cody, called the other afternoon from his Sonoma County home to say howdy and to announce he was mailing two cassettes just out on Relix Records (as in relics), a small but esteemed independent label. I was delighted. George sounded in great shape, rattling on about how great the band is lately, about the return of vocalist Billy C. Farlow, and how much he enjoys playing an established club circuit to a loyal following.

When the tapes arrived I played them immediately. Great stuff. The man is certainly no relic. "Aces High" is a collection of new studio tracks interspersed with deft comedy sketches.

The companion tape, "Sleazy Roadside Stories," contains concert recordings from the early '70s when Commander Cody and the Lost Planet Airmen was a seven-piece ensemble with pedal-steel guitar and musicians who doubled on fiddle and horns. The richer country-western swing feeling, together with the ambience of halls like the Armadillo World Headquarters, works beautifully, especially on the Cody classics "Beat Me, Daddy, 8 to the Bar" and "Hot Rod Lincoln."

Ah, the ol' Commander. Truly one of the great characters of our generation. I met him in Berkeley in 1969 when I was just finishing my first book – about country music – but we didn't become fast friends until our paths crossed six years later here at the beach. During the eight or so eventful years he lived in Stinson, the man provided endless laughter and high jinks, even when times were tough. Seems like only a few years ago that he and the band lived in a house in Seadrift in the front yard of which grew some of the best sinsemilla ever nurtured on the North Coast. *High Times* magazine even ran a centerfold photo of George standing next to a towering specimen of primo Afghani cross.

Cody later moved to a funky cottage in the Calles, then on to the hill. By then he had emerged as one of David Letterman's favorite guests on the comedian's "Late Night" show, usually playing a couple of tunes with the house band. All of which recalls to mind Cody's famous bet with the Sand Dollar's owner Kendrick Rand concerning the former's bar tab which at the time was over $300.

Kendrick, who is a very astute restaurateur, agreed that if Cody could mention the Sand Dollar three times during his next time on Letterman, he would forgive the debt. When word got around the village, the Dollar was packed the night of Cody's appearance.

After playing a short tune, George took his seat next to his host and started off with a bang when Letterman asked him

Oil on canvas by Michael Knowlton.

what he did when he wasn't touring: "I sit at home in Stinson Beach and smoke dope and watch the whales go by and run up my bar tab buying friends drinks at the Sand Dollar." Back here the village audience cheered.

A minute later, while talking about his painting, Cody again snuck in a reference, this one about displaying his canvases at local galleries "and at the Sand Dollar." More cheers here at the beach. The rocker was making it look easy.

But then Letterman introduced another guest and Cody was out of the frame. More chit chat and commercials. Twice the camera panned past George but he couldn't get a word in, let alone a mention. Back here at the Sand Dollar everyone watched in tense silence. We knew the show was tape delayed, but George hadn't called from New York to boast about victory. With less than 60 seconds to go the house band began vamping the show's theme song. Tension ran high.

Finally, just as the screen credits began to roll and the studio audience was applauding, George stood up and shook Letterman's hand, saying, "See you at the Sand Dollar." The stage mics went off the air half a second later. The Sand Dollar erupted in cheers. Kendrick beamed, as well he should. For months thereafter people who had seen the show came into the restaurant to eat and drink and maybe catch a glimpse of the ol' Commander.

September 27, 1990

WEST MARIN FROM A NEW ANGLE

GREETINGS FROM THE SHORE of Tomales Bay. I'm sitting here at my desk in a backyard studio with windows, beamed ceiling and a skylight that promises to be a wonderful office once I unpack the wall of cardboard boxes surrounding me. I'm still getting used to the faint but cozy smell of the Kero-Sun heater, and the slightly higher-sounding purr of my computer's cooling fan, and the different angle of morning sun.

Amidst all this I'm wondering how the Stinson Beach Bong Show went last Saturday night. Early reports indicated the amateur talent show, revived after a decade-long absence, was a smash, playing to a packed community center. In a fitting gesture of hands-across-the-lagoon friendship, the grand prize went to Bolinas's T. Bald Eagle, a fine guitarist, whose ode to Bobo, "Oh, Bolinas" ("where the women want your gen-ius"), brought the house down.

As important, the Bong Show's success is a good sign that the zest and spirit of a wonderful beach community is still very much in evidence, together with new talent and energy.

I feel a touch of longing that I wasn't there for Saturday's festivities, since I was fortunate to have handled the MC chores for the first three years in the late seventies. Those experiences

MC-ing the second annual Stinson Beach Bong Show (1979), here introducing to the packed Community Center talent judge Kendrick Rand who is also Fire Chief and owner of the Sand Dollar Restaurant. A wild and memorable night. Photo: Melissa McMillon.

were the stuff of life memories, but as fate would have it, these days find me in the throes of yet another life experience, this one 19 miles up the coast. Right, after 16 years at the beach, I've moved.

That is, we have moved. After a year-and-a-half courtship involving two residences, Susan and I and six-year-old Bat Baby are now living under one roof near the shore of Tomales Bay. While the change in geographical surroundings is greater than the emotional landscape of an already developing family relationship, nevertheless it's an interesting challenge. For example, it's almost amusing to watch two grown people with decidedly set morning routines make the necessary adjustments to accommodate each other.

While the decision to combine homes was made months ago after due consideration, the search for a new abode didn't begin in earnest until August. At that juncture we very quickly realized that, for us, our beloved Stinson Beach was no longer affordable. Thinking about living elsewhere took getting used to.

Determined to find a new home somewhere in West Marin, we began making the rounds of realtors and telling friends, hoping the latter might tip us to a place before it went on the market. People were very helpful, but looking and waiting was not fun. Next we ran Rental Wanted ads in the *Light* and *The Hearsay News*. The response was minimal, but there was a bright side: As we snooped around Point Reyes Station and Bolinas and Olema and other communities, regarding each as a prospective new home, they all felt great.

Not only did we feel welcomed, there was no sense that we were visiting isolated communities, not even in Bolinas. Instead there was the feeling we were visiting different West Marin neighborhoods.

Somehow, between beating the bushes, making phone calls, trusting our ad in the *Light*—and finally just trusting the ultimate light—we found a wonderful new home. Somehow, too, we managed to combine the essentials of two households into one and move it, all during one exhausting 14-hour day of madness.

That was a week ago. I'm still adjusting to my new surroundings, still filled with immense relief at finding a new home after months of searching. I realize, too, that on several levels I have found a new home. It's been 18 years since a first marriage and this ol' desperado was ready to give up ridin' fences and come off the range.

Happily, too, Stinson Beach is still only 30 minutes away and fond friends remain close by. And while thoughts of the Bong Show linger, I'm looking forward to savoring the delights of our new life on the shores of Lake Tomales. It feels very good to be here.

October 11, 1990

TALKING IN THE DOORWAY

IN THE DEEP OF THE NIGHT along Tomales Bay it is astonishingly quiet. Absent is the soft sigh of waves that is the heartbeat of Stinson Beach which until a few weeks ago had been my home for 16 years. I don't yet miss those wave sounds, for I'm still enjoying the novelty of hearing my ears ring. And noting with amusement that the occasional car passing by the house after dinner may cause me to look up from my reading.

Here 20 miles north of Stinson Beach and 4 miles inland from the sea, and protected from the northwesterly winds by the long Inverness Ridge, I can gaze into the black velvet of a country night sky untainted by the penumbral glow of distant big city light reflected off clouds.

Here, too, with a view unencumbered by Mount Tamalpais, we can sit over coffee at the kitchen table and watch an actual sunrise over the low rolling hills to the east.

But it is quite cold. Ski parka cold. My friend Elizabeth Whitney tells us we're in the local permafrost zone. She exaggerates, but I notice that folks in our neighborhood don't stand chatting in the doorways. Most of the homes scattered in the woody hills hereabout appear to be old vacation retreats of the well-to-do – antique family retainers nestled in the damp shade of overgrown oaks and pine, looking cold and drafty.

A lot are year-round domiciles now. And after glimpsing their interiors and occupants while trick-or-treating with Bat Baby, I sense many of the residents are older, solvent couples with well-traveled pasts and lively inner lives. Many appear to be people of privilege and taste who have eschewed the trappings and bother of visibility while remaining very well connected to the world on their own terms.

I've heard a few people suggest the people here tend to be a touch aloof and snooty, but I have yet to see it. Rather, I sense that here live people who no longer have a great need to be out and about mixing with the world in order to remain very much a part of it. Which must make it very hard on teenagers.

Inverness, for example, is often called Inwardness. But maybe that's because of peoples' reluctance to stand talking in open doorways. Whichever, in the meantime I'm quite happy by the notable absence of BMWs and Spandex.

And happy, too, to take walks along the shoreline of magnificent Lake Tomales. Its secret lies in its mornings. At such times the surface of this narrow finger of a bay is as flat as glass, evoking Lake Tahoe on a calm August morning. The visibility of the water at these times is astonishing.

One such morning recently we ambled along the shore at the base of woody cliffs, encountering little secret coves and inlets, many with aging private docks and floats and rickety wooden stairs zig-zagging up the overgrown embankments leading to the unseen homes above, many doubtless a bit rickety themselves. I imagined summer gatherings of large extended families with lots of laughter and children and sunburned faces and halcyon days that may never have happened but surely deserved to.

Here and there great tangles of fallen trees lay along the base of the cliff, their bone-white branches piercing the slack water, stiff as death even as families of barnacles found purchase on their fingers. We kept an eye out for flotsam and jetsam and admired the movement of a small jellyfish as it laconically flared its skirts, then pulled them in again as it, too, grazed its own watery wonderland.

We dreamed of some day soon packing a picnic lunch and a blanket and tossing them into a canoe and furthering our explorations by water. Splendid idea. In fact, if you happen to have an old canoe you'd like to sell, or know someone who does, please let us know. Of such stuff are dreams made, and columns written. From the shores of Lake Tomales, here's wishing you a rich and warm Thanksgiving, replete with laughter, love and full tummies.

November 21, 1990

WEST WEST MARIN

SINCE MOVING to the Point Reyes Station area six months ago, I've commented about the social landscape of what might be called West West Marin. This is a place where most people work as well as live and where a trip over the hill is less than regular and more than a casual event. Here, too, is a region more vast than I realized, this despite my having called West Marin my home since the mid-seventies.

I admit I'm surprised. Until moving here from Stinson Beach last October, I thought I had a good feel for the terrain. But that was before I had ever walked in driving rain on McClure's Beach, dodging sneaker waves that rolled fast and foamy up to the low cliffs. Nor had I yet stepped inside the old Point Reyes Lighthouse to admire the polished bright work and take a turn on the crank handle that winds its exquisite clockworks. Or walked the sands of Limantour or scented the dry pine air atop Mount Vision, or ambled down the oak-shaded quarter-mile path to the incomparable Tomales Bay cove of Shell Beach.

In contrast to Mount Tamalpais and Stinson Beach, at these scenic spots one seldom encounters more than a very few people. And because Susan and I are early risers, we have more than once savored the calm morning solitude of Abbott's Lagoon and Ten Mile Beach without seeing another soul, to cite just one example.

Moreover, all the rain we've had in recent weeks has transformed all of West Marin into a lush landscape that has given old and familiar views renewed splendor. After five years of drought, I'd forgotten how spectacular these hills look in the green of a wet winter. One recent stormy afternoon as I drove east along Lucas Valley Road past the Nicasio Reservoir, I crested a low rise just as the sun peeked out between showers. There before me was a vista of wet rolling green hills, wisps of cloud grazing the tops of oak and redwood trees, while standing proudly in the center distance was the bell tower of the old Nicasio schoolhouse, all bright red and white trimmed, glistening with rain.

There could scarcely be a better reason for a Sunday drive in West West Marin than to admire such scenes of rampant beauty, unless it was to enjoy driving the '86 Honda Accord Susan just bought to replace the one that was rear-ended last month.

Which was precisely what we did Easter Sunday. On a whim we drove to Marshall and ambled up the Marshall-Petaluma Road onto Bolinas Ridge. For the next 11 miles we drank in the scenery, sunshine and roadside poppies. I confessed I couldn't recall ever being on this stretch of road before. I also admitted I was never precisely clear on the difference between Hicks Valley and Chileno Valley, this despite all those years of reading Sheriff's Calls. Heck, I've still never laid eyes on the Soulajule Reservoir which the Triple A map showed somewhere to our right hidden from view between Hicks Mountain and Three Peaks.

By the gate to Walker Creek Ranch at the base of Hammock Hill we turned left and climbed a beautiful two-lane country road three miles up to the shoulder of Antonio Mountain. There we found ourselves at 1,100 feet looking north at the verdant farmland from Valley Ford to the Petaluma Hills. Sun and cloud shadow played across the checkered pastures and fields. Truly, I've never seen rural West Marin so beautiful.

We drove west along the Chileno Valley Road to Tomales, thence to Nick's Cove for a plate of oysters and a glass of wine. We were pleased to note that proprietor Ruth Gibson has new sweat shirts and menus that proclaim her establishment "the home of the horny oyster (11 out of 12 work)." They've even added a Zinfandel to a wine list which had formerly listed only white and burgundy. This may be the only restaurant in West Marin where the best tables in the house are in the smoking section, which was mostly filled. A fine an unpretentious place, Nick's Cove.

One of these spring Sundays we'll lunch at Nick's, perhaps after we get our first look at the secretive Soulajule Reservoir.

April 4, 1991

MARSHALL-PETALUMA
ROAD

ABOUT THE AUTHOR

A San Francisco native, John Grissim free-lanced for *Rolling Stone* in the seventies before his interests turned to Pacific Rim adventuring with a focus on ships and the sea. He was on the dive team that found the $20 million Spanish treasure galleon *Concepción* in the Bermuda Triangle in 1978. A much-traveled connoisseur of the offbeat, he has written on a wide range of subjects, among them Philippine psychic surgeons, pool hustlers, Hawaiian big wave riders, Australian shark bounty hunters, the search for Bigfoot, and life in backwater Borneo — all while somehow managing to avoid being killed. He is the brother of writer and essayist Phyllis Theroux.

The author of six non-fiction books (a seventh is in the works), Grissim lives in West Marin County where he writes a column for the Pulitzer prize-winning weekly, the *Point Reyes Light*.

COLOPHON

Produced and designed by Michael Sykes at
Archetype West in Point Reyes Station.
One thousand copies printed and bound by
McNaughton & Gunn, Inc., Ann Arbor,
Michigan, in the spring of 1991.
The typeface for the text is Sabon,
and for the titles, Gill Sans Medium.